WHAT PEOPLE ARE SAYING ABOUT

THE LAW OF ATTRACTION

Author Andrea Mathews provides readers with a very thought provoking and insightful examination of the working principles of the Law of Attraction, dispelling the myth that you can get what you want by just thinking about it."

Caroline Myss

Author of *DEFY GRAVITY* and *ANATOMY of the SPIRIT.*

Andrea Mathews brings sense and sanity to the law of attraction, which is one of the most misunderstood concepts in our culture. This is a penetrating discussion of the layers of consciousness that are involved in everyone's life. If you desire greater clarity and fulfillment in your life, this extraordinarily wise book is for you.

Larry Dossey, MD

Author of *The Power of Premonitions.*

The Law of Attraction: The Soul's Answer to Why It Isn't Working and How It Can *points to the real path of transcendence, the real door to the Divine. With this new, radical understanding of the law of attraction, the mystery of your own One Self will open the magic door of life.*

Ivan Rados

Author of *Health It's All About Consciousness.*

Andrea Mathews has given us a wealth of wisdom, insight and new ways of applying ancient knowledge in this wonderfully deep and spiritually sophisticated second-look at the phenomenal global drive to understand the "law of attraction."

Jonathan Ellerby, PhD,

Author of *Inspiration Deficit Disorder.*

Andrea Mathews offers the reader a new, an

understanding and application of the "Law of Abundance." In The Law of Attraction: The Soul's Answer to Why It Isn't Working and How It Can *Mathews explains what most students of "prosperity consciousness" refuse to acknowledge: sometimes the law of manifestation (when insufficiently understood or improperly applied) doesn't work. Mathews then draws from a very deep well of training and experience, blends spiritual and psychological principles, and offers solutions for successfully applying the "Law of Abundance" from a more authentic, spiritual state of mind.*

Michael Mirdad,

Bestselling author of *You're Not Going Crazy . . . You're Just Waking Up!*

The Law of Attraction

The Soul's Answer to *Why It Isn't Working* and How It Can

The Law of Attraction

The Soul's Answer to *Why It Isn't Working* and How It Can

Andrea Mathews

BOOKS

Winchester, UK
Washington, USA

First published by O-Books, 2011
O-Books is an imprint of John Hunt Publishing Ltd., Laurel House, Station Approach,
Alresford, Hants, SO24 9JH, UK
office1@o-books.net
www.o-books.com

For distributor details and how to order please visit the 'Ordering' section on our website.

ISBN: 978 1 84694 495 6

A CIP catalogue record for this book is available from the British Library.

Design: Lee Nash

Printed in the UK by CPI Antony Rowe
Printed in the USA by Offset Paperback Mfrs, Inc

CONTENTS

Acknowledgements

Immeasurable gratitude goes first to Leslie West for her endearing support of both my authenticity and my process of coming to terms with my own explorations of the mystery within me. Each time I touch the hem of that garment, I come away with new information. Her loving warmth and intentional grounding is an invaluable gift for which I am eternally grateful. And I am equally grateful to my children, not only for their adult support of who I am and my work, but also for the many ways that raising them informed me of the beauty and potency of human nature, for they taught me so very much about parenting, about the depths of my own heart and about my own authenticity. I am grateful to my sister, Bonnie Council, for editing some of my earlier work, a lengthy and arduous process that taught me much more about the art of language and communicating my most cogent thought. And I am grateful to my entire family, with all of its dysfunction and poignant mastery of my heart, for all of the lessons in life, love and spirit. I would not be who I am today and therefore could not have written this book without their mastery of my heart or these lessons. Finally, I want to thank my agent Krista Goering of Krista Goering Literary Agency, for her honest feedback, as well as her encouragement, wisdom, guidance and efforts on behalf of getting this book into your hands.

But beyond all of those most personal influences and foundational supports in my life, I would also like to thank all of those mystics, explorers of the human spirit, who have gone before me. They passed through as blind as the rest of us, and yet, with sensitive fingers, touched the mystery and, through that special Braille, learned to see. When I read their work, my own experience is affirmed and enlightened, as I so hope that my work will likewise affirm and enlighten.

This book is dedicated to both the power of mystery and the spirit of exploration in all of us.

Preface

The ideas presented in this book come from years of professional work in which I served clients, workshop attendees, radio show audiences, and readers who continually informed me of their difficulties in working with the current and common understanding of the law of attraction. Through that experience, in combination with my own personal experimentation with that law, I came to know that like any new definition of the depths of experience in mystery, this understanding of the law was both a good start and yet, not enough. In fact, it stops short of offering the very thing it promises—peace and happiness. Much like the Western adaptation of the beautiful Eastern art of meditation, which has so often been reduced to yet another skill to quick-study and execute for optimum performance, the current understanding of the law of attraction has become a struggle, an effort, even a mind-boggling stumbling block for many who are seeking the high road.

Perhaps it was not originally intended to be so, but it has nevertheless become so for many—many who were troubled before taking up the law and became more troubled as a result of this understanding of it. The sad story has begun to be told, in which the human psyche is further split-off from various aspects of itself, fragmented as a result of striving after "positive" thinking and avoiding "negative" thinking in order to attract dreams and prevent "negative" circumstances. This book will not only clarify that story, but it will offer an entirely new perspective on the law of attraction. It does not debunk the law, but it does revise our understanding of it to bring it into the realm of not only the possible, but the probable.

It is absolutely possible for us to attract and be attracted by certain people, places, things, events and circumstances, both desired and undesired. But how and why that happens is not at all like what we've commonly understood thus far.

Introduction

The collective mind has been on a long and winding road toward its ultimate destiny of acceptance. The mystery of our existence, including our collective and individual struggle with the seemingly incongruent and mutually exclusive concepts of suffering and rejoicing, has been very difficult for us to simply accept. And our process has included each one of the stages of acceptance—denial, anger, sorrow, and bargaining—stages that are strangely similar to the now well-known stages of grief, which likewise end in acceptance. Down through history, as we moved through these stages in random and incoherent order, we made up our own mythologies in an attempt to solve the conundrum of life. Through those mythologies we hoped to find the magic bullet that would eliminate our suffering and bring us to a peaceful co-existence with each other and the earth itself. To date, this is an unfulfilled collective soul longing. Yet we continue to hope. So it is that throughout our psychic history we've imagined all manner of superstition that has been intended to give us some modicum of comfort in a world where seeming "lucky" happenstance and random horror can occur at a moment's notice.

We started this process by making sacrifices to the gods who were then supposed to give us a high yield on our crops or enable us to win the next battle with the next unjust force encroaching on our sense of safety. When we saw preferable results, we assumed that we'd done something right, and when we didn't, we assumed we'd done something wrong. We moved slowly from there to organized religions of all kind, which were not only meant to help us recognize and develop a relationship with a higher power or higher way, but they were also meant to help us make sense of our suffering. The sense we made then was based on the same ideal created in the minds of the early predecessors: Being "good" or "doing it right" got good even eternally "good" results, and being "bad" or "doing it wrong" got bad, even eternally "bad" results. Even as these organized efforts were being established and maintained we also continued individual methods of dealing with the conundrums of survival on planet earth, through various magical thoughts and bargains that ranged anywhere from purchasing icons meant to bless and protect, to using voodoo to harm those who threatened.

Now in twenty-first century thought, we have begun to site other causes for our fortunes. Instead of casting aspersions on the gods, we've begun to look to ourselves as both cause and effect, through our current understanding of the law of attraction. This now well-known law erupted into the collective consciousness as a result of the emergence of our combined efforts to blend Eastern and Western philosophies, to explore the human psyche and to continue the struggle to eliminate suffering. Our current understanding of the literature on this law is that it is our thoughts that create our lives. With this new understanding we have come to believe that both "good" and "bad" fortune are attributable to a clear cause. Many of the books and articles on the law of attraction have been read voraciously and have filled us with hope as well as a power struggle between the ego and the shadow for thought dominance. On the one hand, it seems that after centuries of defeat we have finally landed on a solution to the problem of living in a world where suffering can occur. Yet, on the other, the associated power struggle has, for many, become overwhelming and they strive to understand why it is that they simply cannot seem to manifest their dreams. Their frustration has led them to more self-flagellation and attempts to "get rid of ego" or "clear the shadow" as they push ever harder to attain their dreams.

These struggles along with reports of successful manifestation have led many to begin a process of looking within. *But, while the internal view is undoubtedly the right direction, we have not yet begun to look deep enough for the source of our manifestations.* We have yet to understand this law as it works in combination with all of the equally powerful universal laws. Nor have we taken in the full import of what our sacred texts have to say about it. Nor have we understood the impact on the psyche that our current misconceptions about this law are having. For all of these reasons and more, our understanding of the law of attraction must be revised if we are to begin to come to terms with the conundrums of our existence. In fact, our understanding of ourselves must be revised if we are to come to terms with the very nature of that existence.

This book is written to assist us all along the pathways of our individual journeys toward acceptance of who we are and what we are capable of when it comes to getting into the flow of the power of the laws of the Universe, including the *true* law of attraction. What we will learn here is that we are actually a part of those laws, in much the same way that oxygen is a constituent part of air and water. So, while the struggle has been on, over the past several years, to eliminate so-called "negative" thoughts and feelings, even eliminate the ego, this book will serve to eliminate the struggle to eliminate. We will learn how to put ourselves into the flow of Universal law, rather than pushing and shoving ourselves around to force our minds to think only so-called "positive" thoughts. As a result, we may also learn to manifest joy, the highest calling, and the most true life.

This book offers an in-depth understanding of the simplest and most accessible incursion to the flow of Universal energies. It will carry us on an exploration of both a revised version of what it is that blocks us from fulfilling our essential desires, and a revised version of the methods by which we can attain our truest manifestation. What we will find along the way isn't going to be an ego we should get rid of or a shadow we should clean out. It is going to be the final bottom-line energy of Life. The struggle is now over. We can "cease striving" and "know that I AM God." For that I AM is the actuality of the law of attraction.

1

Is Thought Really the Magnet?

In order to answer this question we first have to define thought. And that's going to be a bit hard to do because there are so many things currently defined as thought for which we might change that definition if we considered all the angles. For example, as I am writing this, I am really focused on what it is that I am saying. So, we might say that I am thinking. But the focus is not really thought-based as much as it is what I call *flow-based*. Yes, I am thinking, but before I am thinking there is an underground, almost intuitive place that I am coming from. The words do not come from my thoughts as much as from that deep creative intuitive river. The thoughts seem to come *after* the energy of the flow. When I go back later and edit what I've written, then I'll be thinking. I won't be coming so much from that creative flow as I will from detailed thought.

Further, we say *thought* very often, when we mean *feel*. Quite often in a therapy session, I will ask a client how she feels about something and she will say, "Well, I think...." Or he will say "I feel that...." This is a teaching opportunity in therapy for this is when I will say something like "Okay, that's a thought, but what do you *feel*?" It is clear that the phrase "Well, I think" is going to take us to thoughts, but it is not usually as clear that the phrase "I feel *that*" is going to take us to thought. But when I feel, I don't have a *that*. I feel angry. I feel sad. I feel frustrated. I feel joyous. I feel peaceful. There is no *that* in those sentences. They are simple, direct statements of feeling. *That* will give me a reason or an excuse for a feeling, but it will not define the feeling. For example: "I feel *that* you are going to get mad at me if I tell you the truth," explains why I haven't told you the truth, but it doesn't say how I feel. But I feel afraid. "I feel *that* things are going to go hay-wire unless I do something to fix this" describes the reason behind my impulse to fix it, but it does not define a feeling, which again is fear. Try it, or catch yourself in the act of giving a thought when you mean to give a feeling.

In a given moment there might be hundreds of things of which we are and are not aware, that one could call thought, but which might not really qualify as thought. For example, right now I am typing on my laptop. As I type, however, I am not thinking of each of the letters that I am hitting in order to complete a word and then a sentence. In fact, I can carry on a brief conversation while I am typing. Not a long, complex conversation to be sure, but a brief one can be had even as my fingers are flying across the keyboard. In fact, I find that the less I am thinking about each letter stroke, the better, more accurate and faster is my typing.

I learned from Mrs. Snow, my high school typing teacher, that if I moved from thinking about the key stroke to simply thinking about what I was writing, I would type more accurately and faster. For a while I envied the girls in the class who could type 70 words per minute on one of those old typewriters on which each key stroke took a strong strike of the finger. But they would always say that it was easy and that they put very little thought into it. I knew that it had something to do with what Mrs. Snow had taught us, but I couldn't quite make it happen at first. Yet as I began to implement her theory, I proved it. And as time went by and I had to type college papers and then edit newspapers and magazines and eventually write books, I got faster and faster, and the key strokes took less and less energy as technology improved. Mrs. Snow was right! She was the first to publically introduce me to the mind that functions below the level of thought.

As we examine the features of that world below thought, we have to also consider images. Generally speaking, if someone tells us not to think of a pink elephant, for example, the first thing that happens is that we briefly invent an image of a pink elephant, if only to know what it is that we should not be thinking. But is that image really a thought? Is it possible that we could retain that image without actually thinking of the pink elephant?

Why and how does the mind use images? First, we need to know that not everyone uses images the same way. There is a distinction between those who think first in words that are immediately converted to images and those who think first in images that are converted to words. And that just accounts for the seeing world. Does a genetically blind person create images as a response to a stimulus? So, let's rephrase the question: What is it inside of us that makes us utilize either images, words or something else that is neither, as a response to a stimulus?

It is in attempting to answer this question that we begin to understand the limitations of thought. That immediate response, which is generated less than a nanosecond away from the stimulus—in image, word, or something else—comes from something deeper than thought. Very often we do not even know we have generated this response until we peel back the layers to find it. So, what is it that creates this response that occurs before thought can even grab hold of it?

Actually, there is a constant river of imagery and words that flows below the contents of everyday thought. We can access that river in three ways, through meditation, sometimes through relaxed daily routine, and through sleep. As we become practiced at meditation we fall down into that deep flow of energy beyond thought, which takes the form of images, feelings, intuitions, body sensations or just a soundless hum. Sometimes during a day, if we are well attuned to the inner world, we will slip past thought and into that river. And as we sleep, the dream world is total access to this river of information that flows beneath the conscious mind. So, if thought can be suspended and this flow continues regardless, where does thought stop and that flow begin?

Further, at least certain kinds of thought came about as a result of our need to act according social mores, to become civilized, to fit into a group. Back in the cave man days, that world below thought was much more the modus operandi. Like animals, we didn't use thought as much as we used body function, instinct, intuition and emotion. Yet we survived, and some would say that it was during our ancient days that we were much more closely connected to the Divine. But somewhere back in the fifteenth century, Descartes said, "I think, therefore I am." So, does this mean that the ancients didn't really exist?

Today, we put tremendous stock in thought. In fact, the more well reasoned our words and actions the more highly we are esteemed by others. In the Western world instinct, intuition, imagination and emotion are still more or less relegated to the lower echelons of esteem, though this might be shifting just a bit. But it has been this way for so long that we operate out of the thought archetype as if it were the only feasible way to operate. And yet, I posit the theory that this way of operating is based in just that—an archetype. Thought is something that we, as a collective, have promoted as valuable for so many centuries now that we have developed an unconscious archetype for it. In other words, we all understand thought the same way.

In fact, if you go to Merriam-Webster's Collegiate® Dictionary online for a definition of *thought,* here is what you get:

1a. the action or process of thinking: COGITATION
b. serious consideration: REGARD
c. *archaic*: RECOLLECTION, REMEMBRANCE
2a. reasoning power
b. the power to imagine: CONCEPTION
3. something that is thought: as
a. an individual act or product of thinking
b. a developed intention or plan <had no thought of leaving home>

c. something (as an opinion or belief) in the mind <he spoke his thoughts freely>
d. the intellectual product or the organized views and principles of a period, place, group, or individual <contemporary Western thought>

By permission. From *Merriam-Webster's Collegiate® Dictionary, 11th Edition* ©2010 by Merriam-Webster, Incorporated (www.Merriam-Webster.com).

These definitions represent the common understanding and usage of the word *thought,* but do they really explain thought? For example, do the archaic synonyms, *recollection* and *remembrance* define thought? Reason, which clearly qualifies as thought, is a function of the cerebral cortex, specifically the frontal lobe. But memory—synonymous with recollection and remembrance—involves and is involved in several different regions and functions of the brain. Already we can see that reason is not as global as is memory. Memory can be a part of body sensation, the experience of external events, emotion, thought, space, direction, language, learning and more. And, of course, there are different kinds of memory, including various forms of short- and long-term memory. Many believe that we can have memories about events or facts that did not even occur in this particular lifetime. Most of us know that we simply do not yet fully understand memory, where it comes from or how it works. So, perhaps memory is not thought, but it can form into thought.

Can the power to imagine be called thought, as the above definition indicates? Or, does imagination *form* into thought? Many authors, artists and musicians will tell us that they get into a state of imagination in which either there is no thought or thought is the secondary function, in order to create their finest pieces. And as we've said, many of those who are well-practiced at meditation will tell us that there is a place to which they can go in the process of meditation in which thought is observed, so that the observer is coming from a much deeper place as he observes the thought. And, as we've also said, the dream-state, in which conscious thought is completely suspended, is filled with images or imaginings. So, again we would have to question our common definition of thought.

Now if we go to the verb form of *thought* we get *think* and here's what Merriam-Webster's Collegiate® Dictionary online has to say about that word:

transitive verb

1. to form or have in the mind
2. to have as an intention <*thought* to return early>

3a. to have as an opinion <think it's so>
b. to regard as : CONSIDER <think the rule unfair>
4a. to reflect on : PONDER <think the matter over>
b. to determine by reflecting <think what to do next>
5. to call to mind : REMEMBER <he never thinks to ask how we do>
6. to devise by thinking—usually used with *up* <*thought* up a plan to escape>
7. to have as an expectation: ANTICIPATE < we didn't think we'd have any trouble>
8a. to center one's thoughts on <talks and thinks business>
b. to form a mental picture of
9. to subject to the processes of logical thought <think things out>

intransitive verb

1a. to exercise the powers of judgment, conception, or inference : REASON
b. to have in the mind or call to mind a thought
2a. to have the mind engaged in reflection : MEDITATE
b. to consider the suitability <*thought* of her for president>

3. to have a view or opinion <thinks of himself as a poet>
4. to have concern —usually used with *of* <a man must think first of his family>
5. to consider something likely : SUSPECT <may happen sooner than you think>

   By permission. From *Merriam-Webster's Collegiate® Dictionary, 11th Edition* ©2010 by Merriam-Webster, Incorporated (www.Merriam-Webster.com).

It is true that when we think, we are creating *form*. When we think we are *forming* opinions, considerations, judgments, reasons, or suspicions. But even this definition contains words that don't necessarily match the more refined distinctions necessary to understanding thought. "To have a concern" for instance, though this is a common usage of the word *think*, implies that concerns come from thinking. In fact, concerns typically come from emotions. These emotions may or may not *form* into a thought. A second example: Is meditation thought? As we know, right this second there are countless Westerners out there struggling to suspend thought *so that* they can meditate. So, cogitate, yes; meditate, no.

Now, that was all said to say this: Perhaps there is something deeper that stirs within us, that can *form* as thought, but isn't thought at its core essence. And the question asked in this chapter is this: With regard to the law of attraction, is it really thought that attracts? So now we can ask another: If there is something deeper that has to *form* or congeal into thought, then why is it that we believe that thought is the final magnet?

But if we play with the argument that it is our thoughts that attract, then we have to ask yet another question: Why is it, if thought is the magnet, that not every thought attracts? Well, those who espouse the current understanding of the law of attraction would say that we have to have a thought in a repeated fashion in order for it to attract. But what about those people who are constant worriers, whose thoughts are replete with scenarios of horror that reoccur in their minds daily, even hourly, even moment-to-moment—and yet their worries do not manifest?

When I was a child, one of my chores was emptying the trash into the outside garbage can, picked up later by the garbage men. Many times I would fail to do this chore during the day and end up having to do it at night. This meant that I had to carry the trash through the dark across my long backyard and through a small gateway covered to near invisibility with honeysuckle vines and out into an even darker ally, through which the truck would come the next morning to pick up the trash. Every single time I did this, I was terrified that some man would be lurking around in that alley and that when I got out there, he would overtake me, kidnap and/or kill me. Now this was well before the days in which that kind of thing happened frequently so I don't know where I developed that specific fear. But I will tell you, my thoughts in combination with my emotions had developed a clear story about what was about to happen to me. I knew what this man looked like, smelled like, and sounded like. I knew what it would feel like to have him wrap his odiferous strong arms around me and drag me away. I could even feel my heels dragging on the ground as he pulled me by the neck and shoulders.

I'd start down the back steps with trepidation and by the time I was in the middle of the long backyard, I could feel my armpits prickling with fear. I'd stand outside the tiny opening of the gate to the alley and try to peer over it, under it, around it and through it before I'd enter. And then once I entered, I would throw the trash at the outside container, halfway put the lid on and run like a cheetah back to the safety of my house, feeling that man's hand just behind my ponytail as it blew in the wind of my race with fate.

Now, I gotta tell ya' that's some pretty intense law of attraction work. But there was never, ever a man. While I've written some pretty cool poetry about that fear; and while I still remember the intensity of those nights as if I could launch back into them at a moment's notice—still there has never been a man in the back alleys of my life. So, given all of that law of attraction work, why didn't I attract a man who would kidnap and/or murder me?

Similarly, I've worked with many clients who tell me that they are doing that same kind of work, which includes the powerful thought formations, the intense emotions and visualization work, and yet they have not attracted their dreams. If thoughts are the magnet, even thoughts combined with emotions and image work, then why have these people not manifested their dreams? Well, I do not think it is because the law of attraction itself is invalid—though our current understanding of it certainly may be. But, perhaps we need to go deeper than thought for the answers to these questions.

If we go back to my frightening episodes with my imaginary kidnapper, we can look to all kinds of things. The first, of course, is that I do have a very vivid imagination. And as a child I was raised, as many of us were, in a very dysfunctional home, in which fear and insecurity was fostered, and love, nurturance and security were largely unknowns. So, the fact that I was terrified of some violent doom is not at all surprising to me as I look back.

But just what role does our environment play in our ability to attract the life we want? Over the years of working with people from all kinds of dysfunctional backgrounds I've met many who grew up in extremely abusive environments and even abject poverty. But instead of being crippled by this upbringing, they overcame it. They grew up to be fairly healthy, productive individuals who gave something back to their families and communities. Others grew up to be gang members, drug addicts, or extremely dysfunctional in some other way. They both experienced the same external reality, so what made up the difference? Why did one child grow up to "attract" a good life and the other did not? And why did I not attract some horrible episode of torture that matched my fear of doom, developed in my dysfunctional environment? I say it might have to do with something much deeper than thought, something more akin to identity.

Let's explore this further. Suppose that I would like to have a million dollars. No, let's make it fifty million for good measure. I create a vision board with lots of pictures of money on it, and all the things I'd like to buy with that money. I meditate on it every single morning and every single night and I visualize having that money and what it will feel like to have it. I work hard on eliminating my fear of poverty and my fear of bills as they come in by pretending to myself that as I am writing out my check I'm actually writing a thank you note to the Universe for providing me with so much money that I can pay off all of my bills. I do this and more for a year but nothing shifts at all. In fact, I've had to take a cut in pay, since the current economic crisis has affected my employer. So, what is going on here? Why haven't I attracted the money I want?

Well, the one thing we can be sure of is that there is more going on here than thought alone can answer for. Thoughts are formations made of some deeper energy. The work that I have engaged in as I try to come into compliance with the current understanding of the law of attraction is the work of formations. I have been very busy in the arena of formations, but I am not working at all with the energy that is *behind* the formations. In fact, I may find that the energy that is behind the formations does not agree at all with the formations I am making out of thought.

For example, it is possible that I have not truly explored what it is that I want. What do these millions represent for me? What will I have once I have the millions? We will discuss this more in-depth in Chapter 3, so for now, suffice it to say that one of the reasons I may not have manifested my dream is because I don't really know what I want. But in order to know what I really want, I have to know who I really am.

And so, we come again to the issue of identity. What is my sense of myself as I try to tell someone who I am? Am I impressed more with a sense of myself as firm and implacable, unmoved by the circumstances of life? Or, on the other extreme, am I more impressed with a sense of myself that is empathetic and compassionate? What impact do these impressions have on my desire for fifty million dollars? These self-impressions are part of my identity. Isn't it possible that how we sense and perceive ourselves, how we recognize ourselves could be a forming ground for everything else that comes after that? If this is true then the masks and costumes with which we identify are going to have something to do with what we attract, seek or invite into our lives. And if we live beyond mask and costume into something more authentic—wouldn't this also impact our attractions?

We will talk much more about identity in Chapter 5, so for now, we can just assert again that there is more going on here than mere thought. We are beginning to understand then that thought is limited in its capacity to deliver the goods. Again, this doesn't mean that the law of attraction is invalid. It only means that we must go deeper than thought—our all-too-often futile attempts to *reason* with the Universe—to learn about the true nature of the law of attraction.

And speaking of reason, if in fact it is true, as some think, that the frontal lobe, specifically associated with reason, is the most recently evolved capacity of the collective human brain, but has now become its dominate orchestrating force—what were we doing in the centuries before it evolved? As we look back on our ancestral history we tend to think that the further we go back the more savage, and therefore ignorant, we become. But here I am reminded of the story of Gideon, found in the Christian Old Testament, or the Nevi'im of the Tanakh of the Hebrew Bible in the book of Judges (Chapters 6 through 8).

In this story, Gideon is terrified of a visiting angel, whom he refers to as "Lord" and who is referred to in the text as "God." The angel came to tell him to "deliver Israel from the hand of Midian"(6:13) and assures him that the task will be completed. After several strategies and tests to insure that he really was getting leadership from the Divine, he did begin to consider following the directive, albeit with a great deal of trepidation. Finally, after slowly and with resistance, completing several other tasks, he made a plan to fulfill this calling. He recruited vast armies from other tribes in order to go head-to-head with the Midianites and their allies, the Amalekites. As he camped out with his armies on his way to battle he was stopped by God, who informed him that: "The people who are with you are too many for Me to give Midian into their hands, lest Israel become boastful saying, 'My own power has delivered me'" (7:2). He was instructed to eliminate from his army any man who knelt to drink water, cupping it in his hands to drink. Instead the one who "laps the water with his tongue, as a dog laps" (7:5) would be selected to continue on with Gideon into battle. This left Gideon with 300 men to fight against an army that numbered "as numerous as the sands on the seashore" (7:22).

The ones who lapped the water without cupping it first in their hands were the more barbarian—the ones who had less of that organizing cultural principle of civility, i.e., less rational brain activity. And they won the war. But they did not win the war because they knew how to slaughter the enemy in a more barbarian fashion. In fact, they did not actually fight with the Midianites at all. Instead, Gideon divided them into three groups of 100 each, gave them each a trumpet and a pitcher filled with fire and sent them to three different sides of the Midianite camp. At his signal, they all blew their trumpets, broke their pitchers, and shouted and because God had given the Midianites into their hands, the huge number of Midianites and Amalekites began to run away screaming and fighting with each other.

Whether or not we believe this story to be historically or

otherwise accurate is irrelevant to the metaphor the story yields. The yield is this: Perhaps we need to dance a little more on the wild side. This story leads us to our intuitive and instinctive nature, rather than to logic, reason and thought. All of Gideon's problem-solving and logical strategy got him nowhere. All of our reasoning with the Universe, all of our thought control is not getting us what we really want. Perhaps reason, the most appropriate synonym for *thought,* and a utility of the frontal lobe, is not the brain function that is going to get us to our goal. We might need a more whole-brain, or holistic approach that includes more of our pre-thought capacities.

But the frontal lobe has now evolved into an executive sorter, a decider as to which function of the brain will be used in a given situation. Yet, according to a research article published in 2001 by the National Institute of Mental Health, entitled "Teenage Brain: A Work in Progress (Fact Sheet)," unlike other parts of the brain, the frontal lobe does not fully mature until young adulthood. Perhaps this is why many of us can so easily attest to the fact that children are much more intuitive and imaginative than most adults. I remember distinctly two informing incidents from my own children's lives, which attest to this capacity. One day when I was swinging my three year old son in one of those one chair rope swings, I was stewing over something, lost in thought, as I pushed him absently. Suddenly I heard him telling me exactly what I was thinking. It was quite impressive.

Another more moving incident was when my daughter was almost two. I'd recently had a miscarriage, and in my grief over the loss of that potential life, I'd silently named him Timothy. No one else, not even my husband, knew that name. Within a few weeks of that occurrence, my eighteen-month-old daughter, while pushing a baby doll around in her stroller in the front yard, declared that this doll was her little brother and volunteered that his name was Timothy. Of course, it brought tears to my eyes as I sat down beside her and gave her a long hug and asked her to tell me about her little brother. She simply repeated that he was her brother and that his name was Timothy, as she put her soft little hand on my cheek.

I wonder if these stories would have been the same if my children had already developed the frontal lobe. We all instinctively know that our survival depends on our ability to fit into a world that requires certain things of us. As we grow up in this world that requires more reason and less instinct, more cognition and less intuition, more thought and less emotion, perhaps somewhere in the unconscious realms we do not yet understand, we choose to grow that frontal lobe so that we can choose the reasoning function over those seemingly lower functions of intuition, emotion and instinct or even memory—through which we remember who we really are. Perhaps, unlike Gideon, we choose those who drink water from cupped hands instead of those who lap like a dog, because our frontal lobe is convinced to do so by a society that requires it.

If this is true then trying to get the law of attraction to work for us by working with our thoughts is like working with those men who drink water from cupped hands. In so doing, we miss the miracles. The term *miracle* as it is used here, does not imply a supernatural event, but an über-natural event—the most natural of natural events—those internal and external events that happen every day, often without our notice, until we move into the world below thought. I cannot explain why it is that the Midianites and Amalekites ran away when they heard the breaking of the pitchers, the trumpets and the shouts. But in this story, they did. And I'm only taking this story as metaphor, not as fact. Yet the metaphor is good enough, is it not?

And if we read the rest of the story, we learn that Gideon summoned many other men from Israel to chase the Midianites and Amalekites out of the country and Gideon still had some convincing to do before the people believed in him and allowed him to lead them. But after all of this, Israel had 40 years of peace—the same number of years in which they had wandered in the wilderness before ever arriving in the Promised Land, later called Israel. Yet after Gideon lived many years and had many children, he died, and immediately the children of Israel "did not remember the Lord their God who had delivered them from the hands of all their enemies on every side" (8:34). And so the extension of the metaphor allows us to consider that the über-natural can be forgotten. My theory is that the more we push for thought to be the magnet, the more we are forgetting these miracles.

Having said that, this does not mean that thought is useless and that we should spend our days seeking to be thoughtless. We might not even recognize a message from our psyches if we didn't have the ability to assimilate intuition, emotion, sensation and other energies into thought. So, obviously the power of thought is in its ability to work with the other energies in the mind to give them understandable form. Thought, therefore, becomes part of the process of bringing those energies to consciousness. And that process is a huge part of what we are doing here on planet earth. So, thought is a valuable function, just not any more valuable than the functions that occur before it.

If we apply that understanding to the law of attraction what we can conclude is this: Trying to change my life by changing my thoughts is a bit like trying to change my computer's program by using its keys to type out a letter to myself. And what we are going to learn about the law of attraction as we go is that it will require much more of us than changing our thoughts. But it will also reward us in a much greater fashion than just helping us to fulfill our dreams. In fact, what the law of attraction means for us to fulfill is much higher, wider, thicker, brighter and much more profound than just our dreams—though they may be a small portion of what is fulfilled.

So, to the degree that we are trying to change our thoughts in order to activate the law of attraction, we may be limiting ourselves to far less than what is possible. Further, it is probable that while we are trying so hard to change our thinking, we are simply repressing other thoughts. And this leads us to the next question found in Chapter 2.

2

Why Isn't It Working?

Don't think about that pink elephant! As we said in the previous chapter, thinking about the pink elephant is the first thing that happens when we hear such a command, at least for the length of time it takes to form an image of what it is that we are not to think about. But if we really struggle not to think of it, what will happen? For at least the first few minutes we are going to be trying to get that image out of our heads. After that, in order to succeed, what we are going to have to do is find some way to forget about the whole subject matter. In this way, we will get out of the power struggle by changing the subject.

But if we take that pink elephant and turn it into an intense fear, then we ramp up the anxiety and desire to rid ourselves of it exponentially. So, let's say that I have an intense fear that I'm not ever going to become wealthy. But I know, based on my current understanding of the law of attraction, that this very fear is what is keeping me from being wealthy—which is my intense desire. Now I have intense desire pitted against intense fear. What is likely to happen? More intense anxiety. But because I believe that the current understanding of the law of attraction is true, I will look at that intense anxiety and say that it is attracting *more* things to be anxious about. So, now I think that my struggle is attracting more struggle, and I'm going have to ramp up the energy to win the battle. How will I do that? Just as we had to leave that pink elephant behind in the example above, I'm going to have to find a way to leave behind this enormous and ever-growing anxiety, so that I can begin attracting my desires.

The problem is that in the example of the pink pachyderm, I could fairly easily dispose of this distracting thought by going to do something else. But in order to get my mind off of the intense struggle within me, I'm going to have to repress it. I'm going to have to play all kinds of mind-games on myself to trick my head into believing that I am no longer anxious about my own potential self-defeat.

In order to do this, and since I am following what I understand to be true about the law of attraction, I'm likely to label my anxiety or fear as "ego," with all of its "negative" thoughts, feelings and energy. Simultaneously, I'll be labeling my desire as "higher self" and its thoughts, feelings and energies as "positive." Now the ego is the enemy and I can defeat it by just thinking the thoughts of the higher self. So, I'll start trying to think "positive" thoughts and stay away from "negative" thoughts and "negative" energy. In this way, I think that I am developing my higher self and renunciating my lower self, the ego. But actually I've simply split myself off yet again by pushing my struggle with fear into the unconscious, and replacing it on the conscious level with a much nobler struggle between ego and higher mind. In the process I've failed to notice and utilize the potential treasure that might be found in the so-called "negatives." On the conscious level, however, I'm feeling both "right" and relieved. Whew! All I have to do now is think "positive."

In order to maintain my "positive" thoughts, I'll create a list of affirmations. I'll write these affirmations very carefully so as to not let any "negative" energy in to taint them. They will very often start off with "I am" so as to not add into them the doubt of "I want"—which reminds me that I don't yet have. A few examples:

- I am, right now, buying furniture for my mountain chalet.
- I am wealthy.
- I am fulfilled.

I want to be sure that my affirmations put me in the place of my future dreams; that they allow no room at all for doubt, fear, or any other so-called "negative" energy. And every time I become conscious of these "negatives," I will say an affirmation meant to eliminate the "negative" and keep my mind focused on the "positive." I will continue to affirm and affirm until I have totally changed my mind about my reality. And in so doing, I will attract that new reality—the one I don't currently have. The one I'm not currently living in.

But the problem is that I do still seem to know that I'm living in a reality in which I do not have those desired outcomes. And sometimes my affirmations just remind me of that fact. Sometimes I'm filled with a longing so deep and profound that I ache with the reality of my current situation, because by comparison to my dream, it now looks pretty shabby. But then I curse myself for falling into "negative" thinking and I get back up on the affirmation horse and ride him again. This goes on this way for a while until I find out about vision boards.

I learn now that vision boards can help me to circumvent my "negative" thoughts by building into my affirmations both images and emotions about those images. Obviously, through this process, I must be beginning to get it that it is not just my thoughts that attract but also my images and emotions. And so, I launch into creating my vision board. I imagine all kinds of wonderful things that I am going to do with the wealth once I receive it. I cut out pictures of people skiing, and that mountain chalet I've always wanted, and wonderful expensive restaurants and travel, and I put these images in a collage on my vision board. The whole time I'm building that board, I'm filled with the joy and hope of my dream, and my sense is that just the building of the board puts tremendous attracting energy "out there" so that I can call to myself all that wealth I am imaging.

I decide to go all the way with this thing. I build three vision boards. One for home, one for work and a small one for my car. I'm just not going to allow myself a single "negative" thought. For the first few months, I push myself to get up early every morning and take some time every night to focus on my vision boards and magnetize my wealth. I create visions of wealth coming to me from other people, I imagine wealth landing in my mailbox, I visualize myself living in great wealth. And during the day as I am going through my routine, I thank the Universe every time I think of it, for giving me such great wealth. Further, I refuse to talk to anyone about what I'm doing, for fear that they might discourage me with their "negative" energy. And I keep smiling. After doing this for a few months I begin to have some doubts that it's going to work, but I push, prod and cajole myself not to give up. Sometimes I find myself back in that same old struggle, but I'm determined to keep trying.

The problem is that that damned ego just keeps coming around, doesn't it? And so I curse it, and blame it and tell it that it is not of the higher self and push it around trying to get it to comply. But this isn't as anxiety provoking as it was before I gave this struggle the name of "ego," so I think I must be doing something "right." In fact, I feel now that I am on a noble mission to accomplish the highest I can give to myself and the planet.

But, regardless of whether or not I eventually attain to some part of my dream, have I come one inch closer to knowing myself? What has happened in my psyche as I have launched into my new mission to rescue myself from my current situation? The truth is that I've been so busy trying to force my mind to behave, that I don't know anything else about what I'm feeling or thinking. In essence, I've stopped living my life in order to engage in a battle with my notion of suffering. This means that I really am not allowing myself to find out what treasures are in my current situation, as I tell myself that this situation was created by ego. And, worse than that, I'm steadily blaming myself for not doing all of this good enough.

This is actually no different at base than the struggles that very avid fundamentalist Christians have had with the so-called "flesh" for centuries. Many dear Christian souls spent hours in prayer and meditation trying to make sure that they rid themselves of all sin (read "negative" energy). They tried to cleanse their minds of any thought that was considered to be vanity or blasphemy. They tried to cleanse their emotions of any feeling that didn't appear to be righteous. And they tried to "purify" their minds (read think "positive" thoughts) by thinking only on the highest, most spiritual things. Further, there are many examples down through our collective history of people literally harming themselves physically in order to make the "flesh" behave. They provided for themselves all kinds of painful, bruising and cutting instruments that they attached to their bodies in order to punish it for its humanity. They literally beat themselves with sticks and whips to try to get the body to comply. They did all of these so-called "positive" things in order to be heard by a superhuman God who would then stave off the suffering of potential eternal damnation, and offer them the potential reward of heaven. While we may not be using the literal sticks, whips and instruments of punishment, we are, indeed, punishing the psyche by putting it, unnecessarily, into a battle of Universal proportions in order to stave off suffering and reward ourselves with a "good" life.

I often work with clients who are trying desperately to implement the law of attraction in their lives, by this very method in which they square off against the "ego" as the enemy. They blame, cajole, punish and otherwise mentally and emotionally abuse themselves for having "negative" thoughts and feelings, and they cannot understand why it is that God or the Universe appears to be against them. They are trying so very hard, why hasn't the Universe come to their aid? Is it because they are doing it wrong? Is it because they are not "good" enough? Do they need to "discipline" themselves yet more—i.e., punish themselves more?

When enough of us got to this place in the struggle, we began to hear about the shadow, a concept that has not until recently become one of public consumption but has now been turned into a pop concept. We learned that it was the shadow that created our problems with the law of attraction. First, the ego kept popping up and then the shadow, with its darkest intentions, came around to sabotage us. You know sabotage—it doesn't come around in the light of day, like "negative" thoughts do—it comes around in the dark of night to put the bomb in that airplane. That's what the shadow was doing, and that's why we were not able to manifest our dreams.

But wait. How did that sabotage get into the shadow? All those "negative" thoughts and feelings—where did they go when we told them to go away? Did they just magically disappear? No. They went into the shadow, which is now tripping us up with that same energy we earlier repressed.

This is when I have to stop and laugh at the marvelous wisdom of the psyche, for one way or another, it *will* get our attention. Two simple facts:

1. The psyche is always leaning toward wholeness, so that it uses every aspect of living as fodder for that mission. Thus it is that whatever we push away from conscious awareness, goes into the unconscious, to rise yet again on another day through whatever channel we allow—in order to give us yet another opportunity to chose to bring the unconscious and the conscious together into harmonious union—i.e., wholeness.

2. And that may be just about all we know, if in fact we really know even that, for what we know about the human psyche, you could put into a thimble.

Up until Freud's theories began to come into common awareness, we, as a collective, had not spent much time studying the human mind. He was the first to even begin to help us understand ourselves from the perspective of what has come to be called psychoanalysis. And while some of his theories are now considered by most to be false, if not ludicrous, he was our start. Freud lived from 1856 to 1939. Not so very long ago. We could say that beyond a philosophical understanding, our knowledge of the human mind is limited to what we've discovered over the past 150 years. Considering that we've been here on this planet for many centuries, we have to acknowledge that perhaps we are just on the fringes of our understanding of the human mind.

And our current understanding of the law of attraction is based on that limited knowledge. So, when we talk about controlling the mind, we might be talking about something akin to learning how to ride on the back of a snake. It's a little slippery. And controlling the mind is exactly what we are talking about with our current understanding of the law of attraction. We've begun to believe that if we could just make the mind always think "positive," then we could draw to ourselves all of those external things that we desire. That is mind control.

But the psyche is proving to us through our latest experiments with the law of attraction, that it will not be controlled. In its vast wisdom, it is even with this struggle, moving us to a higher plane of understanding. If it is true that the psyche is always leaning toward wholeness, then when it presents us with a so-called "negative" thought, it is trying to get us to assimilate that into both conscious awareness and a deeper sense of ourselves. So, when we repress it because it is "negative" it is going to appear again, in another form or another channel, *in order* that we might assimilate it.

Our current understanding of the law of attraction has us believing that when this thought appears again it is because it is so powerfully "negative" and stubborn that it keeps coming back up. And we just have to keep fighting it, with "positive" thinking. Then we will have what we want. A big part of the problem here is in our belief that our thoughts and emotions can be categorized into two very opposite compartments: "negative" and "positive."

Within the realm of our current understanding of the law of attraction, a "negative" thought or emotion is any thought or emotion that has all the ear marks of keeping us from getting what we think we want and need. And a "positive" thought or emotion is any thought or emotion that promises to get us what we think we want and need. At base, this is no different from the traditional mindset that originated in attempts to get the gods on our side, by being "good" enough to earn their favor, accompanied by the assumption of "badness" when we didn't seem to earn their favor. Of course, "good" and "bad" were culturally defined then, just as they are now. But as time went by these two very limited categories grew until just about every aspect of living was thrown into one or the other category.

The main feature of these split-off dualities is that they oppose each other and we can define each by its opposition to the other. In other words, it's "negative" (or "bad," or "evil") if it isn't "positive" (or "good" and "right"), and it's "positive" if it isn't "negative." And the whole definition of "negative" and "positive" is based in fear. The only reason we need to divide life up into "positive" and "negative" at all is because doing so helps us to feel as if we can have some say so about our lives—as in whether or not we win the favor of the gods or get the law of attraction to bend our way.

But what if Life—the genuine essence of vital living—can't really be divided up into "negatives" and "positives" any more than the psyche can be forever compartmentalized with no leakage allowed? What do we do then? What if believing that Life and the mind can be divided up into "positive" and "negative" only further stacks the shadow with material that will have to come out later? If we assume that it is our thoughts that create our lives, then shadow-stacking is not a "positive" thing, is it? Further, trying to split ourselves in half this way only sets up a power struggle of monumental proportions within us, in which we damn ourselves for having normal thoughts and emotions, because those thoughts and emotions might be attracting "negative energy."

What is "negative energy?" If we think about this concept, it turns out to be something akin to the old traditional concepts of the devil. And if we study the Greek word for devil, as it is used most often in the New Testament, it turns out to have a root meaning of *the distribution of fortunes*. Of course, that's not how traditional thought has inserted it into our psyches. No. The devil is a personality, a character in the drama of our lives. He is the tester, the thwarter, the "evil" intentions that manifest in the form of harm, loss or "sin." He is everything we could possibly imagine true "evil" to be.

I've often asked those who subscribe to the current understanding of the law of attraction to describe for me what they mean by "negative energy." They explain that "negative energy" is "a force for the dark side." That it is powerful, sometimes more powerful than they are; that it makes them feel dark and it may even make them behave in ways they later regret; that they choose not to be around others who carry "negative" energy because it might get on them; and that they choose not to watch "negative" TV or listen to "negative" radio or read anything "negative" because they fear that they will pick up these "negative" energies. Sounds pretty much like that old devil to me. And yet these same people would insist that they no longer believe in a devil. We are going to be talking more in a later chapter about this whole split between "good" and "evil," but for now we'll just say that if our beliefs have anything to do with what we are attracting, perhaps the belief in "positive" and "negative" thoughts, feelings and energy, should be one of the first to go.

So, of what value are vision boards and affirmations? Well, if the psyche is always leaning toward wholeness, then affirmations and vision boards can help us find out more about who we are as whole people. They might even help us to clarify our truest desires and intentions so that we can then manifest them. But they might not do that in the way we expect.

I see affirmations and vision boards more or less as thought experiments. According to the Stanford Encyclopedia of Philosophy, "Thought experiments are devises of the imagination used to investigate the nature of things" (Brown 2007). So, if I start by experimenting with an affirmation of wealth, then I can use the ritual of the vision board as an investigation into my own true nature. I can listen to how I'm genuinely feeling as I am working on my vision board. I can learn more about the various images of myself with which I have previously identified, comparing them to the image that is created in my mind when I say my affirmation or look at the image I've pasted on my vision board. Are they the same or coming from the same place from which I created the mask and costume I've always worn? Or, do they come from my authentic Self? In this way I can begin to distinguish between fantasies essential to a role I've played in life, and true desires. Thereby, these thought experiments help me to identify with my truest essence instead of a twist on the agenda I accepted from my family-of-origin and my culture as identification. This is very different from trying to control my thoughts.

If, for example, my desire for wealth is related to an "I'll show you" mentality based on the fact that I came from poverty and was mocked and ridiculed for that as I grew up; then I might need to question whether or not this desire is genuine to the authentic Self or soul, or if it is merely a further affirmation of myself as somehow less than others. If, through my thought experiment, I learn of my "I'll show you" agenda, then I may need to go back to the drawing board to find out more about what's under that agenda.

Because our current understanding of the law of attraction is so tied up with money, or our ideas about wealth, self-guidance can be very confusing, without the use of exploratory tools, such as affirmations and vision boards. This is true because we forget that once upon a time there was no such thing as money. Our current economic system is something that we have collectively created to cope with the potential for suffering and inequity. But in grade school we learned that the first form of exchange between humans was the bartering system in which we traded objects of desire. Someone wanted some property he didn't have, so he traded some property he did have for this other thing he wanted. This gave him a modicum of control over his frightening security issues. Owning property was one of the methods we used over time to keep down the level of suffering in our lives. The more property we owned, the less likely we were to starve or be homeless. Slowly we built money into the trade negotiations, so that if we wanted something to own, we traded money, instead of an object or a service. And we have built the rest of the structure since that time. Now, it is money that gives us that same sense that we have some measure of control over the potential for suffering in our lives. The more money we have, the less likely we are to suffer starvation, homelessness and other less obvious traumas. We can see then that money is a method by which we stave off the demons of suffering.

It has, in that sense alone, become a psychological rabbit's foot that we rub to keep ourselves feeling safe to some degree. Because over time we needed to really trust that rabbit's foot, we began to build more structures around it. We built cultural restrictions and privileges based on the amount of money we had. So, if you had money not only were you allowed certain things, but you were prohibited certain other things. You might have a grand home, but your manners and social face must be without reproach. You were held to a higher standard than the mere plebeians who struggled for their food. Their savagery might be tolerated, but no such toleration would be allowed for those with money. And over the years, money took on even more power, as it became attached to politics, health and even religion.

Now, that psychological rabbit's foot is tied to everything we deem important, so that when we set out to work with the law of attraction, we just assume that money must be a natural part of the equation of happiness. This makes both money and happiness quite confusing topics. And it gets even more confusing when we get psychological issues, such as money-as-power, money-as-love and shame related to backgrounds of poverty, thrown into the mix of compulsive wants.

Actually, money isn't natural at all. It is a contrived gadget that we created to negotiate life on a planet on which suffering can occur. Nor is money the root of all evil. Money is neutral in value—a means to an end—of no more value than the button we push to page an elevator, or the hammer we use to build a house. Money gets us something. Affirmations and vision boards are two of the many tools we can use to help us find out what we want that something to be. Used as thought experiments then, vision boards and affirmations can be instruments of clarification that help us to get closer to the truth of both the roles we play and the authentic Self.

But to the degree that affirmations and vision boards are insisting that we only think "positive" thoughts and have "positive" emotions, our affirmations and vision boards are actually working against us. They keep us split-off from gold-minds of information about ourselves that only so-called "negative" thoughts and emotions can give us. And they serve as yet another method we use in our strategic efforts to avoid feeling our feelings and knowing ourselves.

So-called "negative" thoughts include, doubt, uncertainty, thoughts of unworthiness, confusion, complaints, thoughts related to fear and more. But each one of these can be extremely useful in helping us to investigate ourselves, and in helping us to traverse the regions of the unconscious, bringing back home to conscious experience all manner of treasure. Let's consider these.

Doubt is the precursor to all true knowing. Doubts call us to question and examine life in a way that allows us to develop original thought. So, if I doubt that I can manifest wealth, but I tell myself that I shouldn't have that doubt and I repress it, then not only do I miss the opportunity to understand myself and know my capacities better, but I am just postponing the inevitable return of that same doubt. If, on the other hand, I embrace that doubt then it becomes the motivation for asking the right questions. If I examine my doubts, I might find that my doubts don't believe that I can manifest wealth *because* of something: *Because* I've never had wealth, *because* I don't have a plan, *because* I don't comprehend wealth, etc. Those *becauses* give me an inroad to my own psyche. For example, I can learn to sit with not having a plan and find out if my lack of plan is actually related to the possibility that I really don't want to put much energy into gaining wealth; but, for example, I'd rather put my energy into building relationships. This may allow me to change my life plan to something much more authentic to me.

Further, as I experience my doubts this also sets me free to experience the whole journey from lack of fulfillment to fulfillment. If I didn't doubt, I would not have the experience of the doubt and would not therefore, gain the experience presented by answering the questions doubt presents. It is our experiences, *not* our intellectualizations, from which we gain all that life has to offer us. Trying to control my thinking is an intellectualization—not an experience.

Uncertainty is another supposed "negative" thought. And yet uncertainty is an aspect of every single and plural element of living, for it points to all the myriad unknowns. In fact, there is not much that we do actually know for certain. To remove uncertainty from thought, therefore, would be to remove the mystery from all of life. But we are uncomfortable with universal mysteries. We want to solve them.

Our solutions, however, are often based in mythology—

which of course they must be, because what else but mythology would have the temerity to try to solve such mysteries? The best we can do with such mythology is to put a tarp over mystery so that we cannot see it anymore. Our mythologies are but bargains with mystery, in which we say to ourselves: "IF I believe this, THEN I'll feel safe and secure." We'll speak much more about bargains in a later chapter, but for now, all we need know is that mystery is something we can learn to accept as a part of the wonder of living.

Have you ever stepped out of the light long enough to see the millions of stars within and beyond our galaxy? The best place to see that is in a campsite or a rural setting with very little light around. I've only seen the night sky utterly filled with stars a few times in my life and it was simultaneously completely spectacular and totally mysterious. The interesting thing about this experience, however, is that the first thing we tend to do in the face of such enormity is try to find the stars and constellations we already know—constellations made up of mythology.

There is a comfort in thinking we know. So, finding Mars, Venus or Orion in the night sky, takes a little of the edge off of the uncertainty that is apparent as we gaze into the silent distance and see stars light years away that probably don't even exist anymore. What mystery lies between those stars and us? Do even our strongest telescopes tell us the spiritual meaning behind these stars? Where is the end of the universe? Mystery and uncertainty is apparent to us as we step out of the light into the sweet silence of the night sky. And the more we allow ourselves to step out of the light of so-called knowing, and into the uncertainty of mystery, the deeper we accept ourselves as beings of mysterious depth and power. We cannot sense our power and depth if we are busy trying to control our thoughts because we fear that if we think "negative" thoughts they will attract something "negative," or at least block us from having our more "positive" dreams. Uncertainty or leaning into mystery means letting go of control.

But how about thoughts of unworthiness? They can't possibly give us anything "positive," right? Thoughts of unworthiness are not merely thoughts. They are an extremely intelligent mix of belief, feeling and thought that add up to identity. And the thoughts are just the tail of an otherwise invisible donkey. So, unless we are spending our energy trying to pin the tail on it, then we've missed the point entirely. We will have much to say about identity as we go, but for now, we'll just say that if we listen to the thoughts of unworthiness as they present themselves to our conscious awareness, this gives us the opportunity to uncover that invisible donkey of identity and begin to put it to work, carrying us to Bethlehem where we will birth the Divine child that is the authentic Self. In order to live more true to who we are, we have to also uncover the beliefs and identities that are not true to who we are. We cannot do that if we simply treat anything that might lead us to those beliefs and identities as a "negative" to be avoided.

Confusion is another so called "negative" thought, but one which can be a true treasure trove, for it is often made of an inner conflict between two objectives. One of these objectives is often favored by the unconscious and the other by the conscious. This means that unbeknownst to the conscious world, the unconscious has an agenda that it would like for us to fulfill. But the conscious world has another whole agenda. We tend to think that this means the unconscious wants us to do something bad or to fail, while the conscious mind is striving for goodness and success. But actually it could mean that the unconscious is holding a specific authentic need or desire that has been unaddressed, and therefore, sent into the realms of the unconscious, while the conscious identity is striving to please others and doesn't want to know about that very legitimate desire or need. So, if I embrace my confusion, then I might find insight that will help me to get clear on who I am and what I desire. Who I am and what I desire are going to be the keys to the power of manifestation.

It is very interesting that we tend to believe that we can spend the first half of our lives staying *out* of touch with who we are and what we truly desire, and somehow just because we are now trying to obey the law of attraction, we are going to land just the right jobs and the perfect relationships without ever having to find out who we are and what we truly desire. Very often I work with clients who tell me "I know myself pretty well." But as we are working together I will inevitably have to ask them how they feel about a particular given or what they think of it, and they will respond with, "I don't know." If they do that frequently, I will eventually gently confront them with the fact that to the degree that they say "I don't know" to the myriad questions about what is going on inside of them, that's the degree to which they do *not* know themselves. And an unknown Self is an unknown manifester.

Or, what about our complaints? With the current understanding of the law of attraction, we tend to believe that complaining is a sign of ingratitude, and that it will only bring more "negative" energy into our lives. But what if my complaints were actually telling me about all of the things that I have built into my life that are not working for me, because they don't actually come from my authenticity. Wouldn't knowing my own complaints help me to declare and then manifest my authenticity? If for example, I am very unhappy in my current job, but I just tell myself that I need to get a better attitude, then I am not likely to put much energy into considering what I'd really like to be doing. I might even call myself a wimp, tell myself to get over it and just grow up. Think "positive," I might say, and "positive" things will come your way. But I'm not likely to attain my truest desires if I cannot see the backdrop of those things I do not desire.

And finally we have those thoughts that are related to the emotion of fear. Fear has become, to most New Age/New Thought believers, the intellectual and emotional equivalent of

Satan himself. Fear is the bottom-line worst possible thing we can feel. What we fear so much about fear is its seeming power to remove from us the object of our desire. But what we can't seem to see is that we have made fear into this demonic force, *because* we are afraid. If we could receive and embrace our fears, then they would have no power to dictate our lives.

In fact, our thoughts of fear are conscious expressions that can lead us to a boatload of information, found in the emotion of fear, about who we are, what we want and how we are thinking of getting it. Suppose, for example, that I am afraid of success, and yet I am yearning for success. This is a common conflict that often creates two other seemingly "negative" thoughts: doubt and confusion. If I try to stave off my fear of success it will just go underground and pop up again in some in-your-face kind of way that doesn't allow me to miss it, so that I may choose eventually to deal with it, thus becoming more whole. Or, I may just choose to send it into the unconscious yet again. But if I embrace it, it can help me create the life I want.

How can this be? Well, my fear of success is there for a reason. Perhaps, for example, it is based on the fact that when I once was successful, in becoming high school President of my class, I took responsibility for all kinds of things over which I had no control and found myself not only burned out but quite embarrassed. But now, if I embrace this fear, telling it that it is okay to come forth into the light and let me look at it and even love it, then I'm likely to find that my fear of success is a handy tool I can use to change my life.

Now I can examine what happened in high school and come to some new conclusions about its meaning. I might come to understand that I have this pattern in my life of taking responsibility for things I cannot control. I cannot, for example, control how others feel about my decisions, or how they feel about me. I can't control what others do, or say or think. If I find that my "lack of success" in high school was related to my attempts to control others, then I can begin to assimilate the fact that this was not lack of success at all, but a misguided attempt to do the impossible. Now that I know that, I can begin to see that it isn't success that is the problem, but the pattern. As I gain clarity, I can create a better plan to live more authentically.

So, we can see that so-called negative thoughts are only powerful to control our lives to the degree that we do *not* embrace them. The more we push them away, in fact, the more control they have, because they are going to go down into the unconscious where we can't see them sneaking around trying to sabotage us. And the more we push them away, the more energy we are going to have to put into keeping them in the unconscious—which means that there is just that much less energy for living authentically and fully. Further, staying in that rarified world in which no "negative" thought is permitted keeps us from experiencing all of life, all of its deep profound beauty.

Our so-called "negative" thoughts often spring from so-called "negative" emotions or feelings. Emotions like pain, sorrow, anger, and fear. Each of these emotions has value not only for the buried treasures held within it, but also because it brings us to a place of mysterious but often poignant beauty. If we have suffered a tragedy in life, if we really allowed ourselves to feel, we understand the pain and sorrow of that tragedy. If we allowed ourselves to sit with, feel and then soothe those feelings we know that as we just come off of a crying jag, we find more beauty in the color of the grass around us. The sky is bluer and people's words and actions mean so much more. We know that even as the pain surrounds us, if we can sit with it and allow it its say, we simultaneously feel a deep peace as we are able to walk into the cold, dark caverns of our own being and light a fire there.

We swim the ocean depths when we range the full extent of our feelings. And these depths make it possible for us to see and fully appreciate the wonder of life. Perhaps it will not always be so, but for now, the truth is that nothing else, thus far in our evolutionary experience, has been able to bring us to those depths, like so-called "negative" emotions can. Unlike so-called "positive" emotions, pain, sorrow, fear and anger make us pay attention. Even if only for a brief time, we begin to ask the right questions. Yet even anger and fear do not have the impact that pain and sorrow do to bring us to new consciousness and even new heights of transcendence. Still, we resist these emotions.

I put sorrow and pain together here because they are slightly different and yet seem to come together in a dance with every grief experience of any kind. Sorrow is that sense that we long for something or someone we have lost or wish we'd had. Pain is that bolder sitting on the chest that doesn't let go until we stop and breathe it in. Pain is the ache that goes with the longing of sorrow. We fear these two as if they were the bubonic plague.

In fact, many of us are depressed simply because we don't want to feel pain and sorrow. Now, most depressed people will tell us they do feel pain and sorrow. But very often, they are feeling only the fringes of it. The rest of the time they are feeling the hopelessness and loss of energy that comes from trying not to be overwhelmed by the deeper aspects of that pain and sorrow. That takes a lot of energy, so that finally they get exhausted and can't seem to get out of bed. The more we deny ourselves access to the richness of the feeling world, the less we feel alive, the less interest we have in living, the less we want to get up in the morning. And the simple fact is that once we start repressing feelings, we don't just repress the so-called "negative" ones. We repress all of them. This is work. And it just takes the steam out of our ability to really desire life.

Whereas, if we would simply embrace the sorrow and pain, not only would they go away faster, but we wouldn't have to add depression to them. All too often ***de***pression is simply ***re***pressed emotion. In order to resolve this kind of ***de***pression we have to begin to ***ex***press the ***re***pressed emotion. In that process we are going to have to feel the sorrow and pain we were trying to avoid in the first place. So, here's the deal: Feel it now or feel it later. One way or another the psyche intends to carry us there, and in so doing, introduce us to ourselves at a whole new level.

Only those of us who have actually done the work of embracing sorrow and pain can tell of the riches found there. And there are many, such as a whole new appreciation and acceptance of life on life's terms, a deep compassion for self and others and a newfound strength to endure. But the best thing that comes out of diving these depths is a knowledge that we can dive these depths and not only survive it, but become more fully alive because of it. Ever after having gone to the depths of such darkness, we know that, no matter what happens, we'll be okay. In that way and others, darkness brings us to the light. So, avoiding or denying our sorrow and pain only robs us of the very treasure we are seeking through so-called "positive" thinking.

Anger seems easier to feel than sorrow or pain, but has its own "negative" connotations. We don't want to be seen as "angry people." We want to be seen as "nice" people. So, we tend to deny our anger in many different ways. For example, as we are working on anger in therapy I find that clients will frequently say, "Oh, I wasn't angry. I didn't yell or throw anything." I often respond with, "Well, did you *feel* angry?" Oh yes, they felt angry, they admit, but they weren't really angry because they didn't *act* angry.

Another way to deny anger is to deny its various levels. Frustration, irritation, madness, fury, coldness and rage are all different levels of anger. So, I hear people say, "I wasn't angry, I was just frustrated." Or, "I wasn't angry, I was just irritated." Some push anger to cold calculation, because feeling or showing anger is showing vulnerability. We do all of this and more because we wish to minimize our awareness that we are angry, because our worth is in some way diminished or threatened by it. So, a good solution to this dilemma is to blame the other guy. Now my worth is not diminished, yours is.

The truth is that anger, like any other emotion, is just a message *to* us, *from* us and *for* us. Our emotions are our internal messaging system. They inform us of how we are responding to a given situation, event, person, place, thing or to our own internal world. They give us huge amounts of information about our experience, and could even tell us about our next best step if we listen to the deeper aspects of an emotion. But our current understanding of these emotions, relative to the law of attraction, is that if they are "negative" they should not be felt. If they are felt, they might damage permanently our visions for our future. What a double-bind we have put ourselves in! If exploring my emotions could help me know the next best step, but I won't explore my emotions because they might keep me from getting what I want—I'm pretty much damned if I do and damned if I don't.

Anger tells us that there is a problem somewhere that needs a resolution. The resolution is not to pretend that we are not angry and it is not to go beat someone else up. The resolution is going to be found in sitting with the anger, listening to everything it has to say and then allowing ourselves enough time to process through what we've heard and come up with a plan of action to which we can authentically commit to solve the problem. The problem will not, however, be found in someone else's actions—much as we might want to find it there. The problem will be found in our own. So, the plan of action will have to do with changing our own behavior in some way. Now, that change may entail communicating better with someone else. It may even entail moving ourselves out of the proximity of someone else. But it won't entail taking responsibility for and trying to change someone else's behavior by telling them what *they* should do to make *us* feel better.

We discussed fear earlier, but let's go a little deeper now. Fear has the potential for bringing us to the depths of our vulnerabilities so that we can see all of the soft, sweet, yet powerful tissue of the Self that needs our focused attention. Fear is the little child within us that needs our comforting stabilizing hand. It is the part of us that wants to crawl up in our laps and be assured that life is good and safe. The problem is that rather than assuring our fear that life is good and safe, we insist that it stop yammering and whining. We tell it to shut-up. Thusly, we make it more afraid.

This is the way of fear: It exposes us to our tenderness, and that very tenderness becomes our strength because it is in walking compassionately with our vulnerabilities that we learn to put up appropriate boundaries, speak from our protective anger, and adjust with grace to new and strange environments. If we never felt afraid we would never know that we needed to do such things to take care of ourselves. I have often found it to be true that those people who come to see me for therapy, and say that they don't want to feel the "negative energy" of fear, are the very same people who have boundary issues and an inability to self-soothe.

Fear is a profound messenger, for though it is not always telling us that we truly have something to fear, it does expose us to our own soft underbelly. And it is that soft underbelly that will be the sweetest and most essential part of our being, not only because we now know how to protect it, based on what we've learned about what it needs; but also because it is so essential. That soft underbelly is the place of our gentlest peace if we can allow ourselves to go there. And our first inkling that we are being permitted to go there is in that first feeling of fear. Listening to and embracing fear leads us to the place that we will ever-after find to be very dear and sacred.

But we also fear feeling our angers and fears, because we are afraid we might act on them. Yet we can see here that the process of listening within is one in which we suspend action long enough to listen and genuinely hear. As we listen we hear all the layers of a particular feeling. We hear its surface reactivity; the voice below that reactivity, which can tell us about a given problem or an internal distortion; and we hear the energy below that, which is simple, pure energy. As we sit with non-action and simply hear all of the different layers of a particular emotion, we are gaining tremendous amounts of spiritual information. And it is not until we sort through this information that we act. At that point our action is much more likely to be based in the soul's intention.

So, we can see that those so-called "negative" thoughts and feelings we are trying so hard to avoid are actually leading us to who we truly are as Divine Beings. They are *not* who we are, but by becoming aware of them, we can learn of who we are. If we are going to attract anything, wouldn't it be best to attract from our truest, most authentic Self? Ultimately, what we are saying is that by avoiding "negative" thoughts and feelings we have put ourselves in a place of strife and struggle. In fact, it is that very striving and struggling that is a central problem with our current understanding of the law of attraction. All the while we are struggling against the "negative" and striving for the "positive," we are not only splitting ourselves off from some of the very sources within us that would help to facilitate our desires, but we are struggling and striving.

In so doing, we are basically living in a state of arrested fear. We strive and struggle because we fear that we will not get what we want unless we do. We strive and struggle because we are afraid we won't be able to quiet the "negative" voices within us. We behave according to the dictates of our fears, because we are certain that if we don't our worst fears will come true. We are living in fear, as we strive to imagine all the "good" that is about to come our way. And all that is accomplished is the growth of the fear. Even if we go with the current understanding of the law of attraction, how would we manifest our "higher self" that way?

But there is another understanding of the law of attraction about which much more is yet to be said. For now, what we need to know is that the struggle and the striving is a problem meant to be resolved, not meant to be promoted. In order to manifest the Self we have to know who that Self is. And in order to know who that Self is, we have to "Cease striving and know that I AM God" (Psalms 46:10). We can read that command this way: "I must cease striving in order to know that I AM God." In order to know that we are Divine Beings, we have to cease striving. All of our vision boarding and affirming will not bring us to this knowledge unless we can do the vision boarding and affirmations from a place of effortless effort.

Effortless effort is getting into the flow. It is that place in which we are totally unified. Every aspect of our being is working in harmony with every other aspect of our being. We are congruent and whole. When we act with effortless effort, we are not striving and struggling. Rather, we are smoothly and, without any effort or struggle, just doing. We tend to think of activity, behavior and doing as coming from effort. There's a have to, a should, an ought, a push, a pull, a struggle to get energy moving or to stop it from moving. There's the use of all of those muscles and thoughts and feelings. But here we see that there is a way to use all of those same muscles, thoughts and feelings without any effort whatsoever.

Many of us have experienced this if we think back. Perhaps we have risen in the night to the cries of an infant or child and with a heart full of compassion and love, stayed up for an hour or more with our child, changing, feeding, rocking, and gently putting the child back to sleep. We weren't even thinking of being tired, or how tired we might be in the morning; we were just all one piece moving in the same direction in the flow of love. Of course, we also remember those times when we were thinking of how little sleep we were getting and it felt like getting up and tending to the child was a tension grinding in our chests. This is how we can tell the difference between being in the flow and being in the struggle. That grind tells us we are striving. That smooth simple unaffected energy tells us we are in the flow.

The hero is in this flow when he sets out to rescue someone. He's generally not thinking, "Oh dear, what if I get killed?" or "Should I go now, or later?" No. He sees something that needs to be done, his compassion, his brain and his muscles kick into gear at the same time and he sets about the task without effort. The next day his muscles may be terribly sore because of the enormity of strength he had to use to accomplish his task, but he wasn't thinking of sore muscles at the time; he was thinking of what needed to be done. The mind, body, emotions and spirit were all set to the same channel—the flow. Now, of course there are also those times when we second-guess ourselves in a crisis and we feel terribly afraid and indecisive—this is when we are in the mind-set of striving.

So, our current understanding of the law of attraction is skewed along the lines of this striving—even as it is insisting that we let go of results. In order for us to know and live into and out of our own power, we must cease striving. But this is where that E-word comes back into play, doesn't it? Ego. That nasty old devil is at it again, interfering in our plans to have our dreams! And so the advice we get from well-intended friends who are relying on the current understanding of the law of attraction is, "You just need to get rid of that ego."

I want to be very clear here, so I won't mince words: We absolutely should ***not*** be trying to get rid of ego. The ego is an essential component of the psyche. In its healthiest form it is a liaison between the inner and outer worlds. Without the ego we would have no negotiator; we would not be able to put bones to our sense of self in the world; we would not be able to distinguish reality from delusion, and phantom ghosts of thought and imagery would just be allowed to flood in over us and take control. In the mental health field we say that those who lack ego-strength are those who are most vulnerable to psychosis. Ego allows us to set ourselves upright and ground ourselves in the world.

We absolutely need the ego to be planted firmly within our psyches and to be given power to liaison between our deepest selves and our outer worlds. But much of the current New Age/New Thought thinking tells us that ego is the problem and that we need to get rid of it. In trying to wrap our minds around this thinking, we label the ego with all manner of issue with which we are burdened, such as pride and self-loathing. Then rather than compassionately embracing and loving our pride and self-loathing into understanding, we create yet more pride and self-loathing by trying to split-off from them, blame, ridicule and belittle them.

Here's how that works. If I hate myself, it is usually because at a very young age this was my solution to having been rejected in some way by significant others, usually parents. In other words, I agree with them, that I am despicable, thus keeping myself in a strange alliance with them, based on the frightening prospect that I need them more than I need myself. So, now as an adult, if I'm trying to follow the current understanding of the law of attraction, I realize that self-hatred, which I assume to be generated by ego, is getting in the way of the attainment of my desires. So, I begin a campaign against ego. Now, I hate my hatred of myself and I am constantly frustrated by my continued self-hatred. Nothing has changed, for I have now just allied myself again against me.

The same is true of pride. Excessive pride is simply a coping mechanism for feelings of excessive inferiority. So, as I battle with my pride, I'm only going to set up one of two polarized possibilities. I'm going to increase my pride as I battle against it and feel more and more proud of my efforts at self-control. Or, the more likely possibility is that in the process of battling with my pride, I'm going to run into my inferiority and have to develop more pride to compensate for it.

These are not really issues of ego. They are complexes with which we have identified. An identity is an ego-state, but it is not the ego itself. An ego-state is a way of negotiating between the inner and outer worlds, by hardening into a mask, a costume, and a certain way of living, called a role, in order to respond to a difficult reality. So, if I'm raised in a home in which both of my parents are drug addicts, I might need to become Superwoman or Superman just to stay alive. And the miracle is that I can actually pull that off. So, I do. I take care of the house, raise my younger siblings and even pay the bills when I have to. This Super-identity is an ego-state. From this ego-state, or mask and costume, I live out a role that performs in certain designated ways. In its most extreme form this role can act like a caricature. But it isn't who I really am—it's just who my family and I thought I needed to be in order to stay alive and attached to them.

The ego creates states when it has to negotiate between inner and outer worlds that do not match—i.e., it tries to match the outer rather than the inner world. Ego-states are adaptive in nature. When we took on an ego-state, as a way of coping with our environments, we went into an altered state of consciousness. You might even say we hypnotized ourselves into believing that we were someone other than who we really are in order to survive or stay attached to significant caregivers. In order to understand this a bit better we might think of the ego-state as a literal role in a play or movie, with which we permanently identify. Though over time this role becomes so familiar that it begins to feel quite natural, of course, it isn't who we really are. Yet because it does feel natural to us, it can be a bit confusing to start thinking that there is another part of us that is *truly* natural—and that it is Divine. But, if we are going to attract the truest things of our truest Self, we can't be living in a state of consciousness or a state of being—even if that state is well-being. We are not looking for a state of being. We are looking for *Being* itself.

So, no, we don't want to get rid of ego, but we will eventually have to come out of the ego-state that dominates our sense of ourselves in the world. Ego is not the enemy, but neither is an ego-state the answer. Ego is meant to serve a healthy purpose. My healthy ego allows me to go deep within myself and make room for me to live fully in this body and this mind as me and then it allows me to carry that "me" out into the world. It allows me to negotiate with a world that might be very different from me, without giving myself up for it. When we get into an ego-state, however, we give ourselves up for our world.

And this is exactly what we do when well-intended but misguided spiritual advisors tell us that, in order to have what we want, we have to get rid of ego. This is but a trade, and not a very good one. And behind that trade comes all manner of equally bad trades. For example, we trade connection with the world for an attempt at some rarefied state of bliss, by refusing to watch, listen to or read any news at all. And in so doing we end up ill-informed about all manner of things from recalled medicines to economic information that would be helpful to us. And worse yet, we trade in our discernment for the New Age advise that tells us that we should not "judge" the toxic people in our lives, but rather "see them as healed and whole," and stay by their side to "help them." In so doing, we may be trading discernment for denial and blindness, which means we miss this unique opportunity to change entire psychic structures of attraction to old paradigms. We might have been drawn and drawn ourselves to these toxic people in order to work though unresolved issues from childhood, which will finally be resolved when we make clear decisions to move out of striking distance of their abuse or venom. We can then choose, if we still wish, to see them as healed and whole—from a distance.

Essentially, this misguided way of dealing with life and its struggles is an effort to live in another world from the one in which we are being challenged to live. It tells us that our world and even our lives are illusions. Taken literally this philosophy amounts only to denial, and how will denial help us to evolve?

What if the challenge of living in this world, just the way it is *is* our evolution? What if the world and our own maladaptive responses to it *are* what we are working through in order to evolve to the truest essence of our Beingness? Would ignoring and denying the world as it is then help us to evolve? Would pretending that the ego is the enemy help us to evolve? Would splitting ourselves off from varying aspects of ourselves? *How does refusing to dive for the treasures found only in the oceans of our own psyches help us to better garner the treasures of the external world?*

We were not meant to live in a struggle with ourselves. Nor were we meant to live on some rarefied plane of existence in which we are not really a part of the community of beating hearts and messy mistakes. We are meant to be here now. Really be here now. Here. In this. Just as it is. And in that very messiness, and blood driven heart motion, we are meant to find life. LIFE. Can we do it? Well, we might first need to know a little more about what we want in this world.

3

What Do We *Really* Want?

The law of attraction is fundamentally based in desire. In fact, without desire the whole need for a law of attraction falls apart. But the problem with using desire as a springboard for attractions is in distinguishing it from all of the other things in the human psyche that look like desire. So, in order for us to get a clear definition of what desire is, we are first going to have to get a definition of what it is not.

For example, I might want to consume a big fat juicy steak every single night of the week, with three or four glasses of red wine and a load of pasta. Is this my truest desire, or is it a compelling want? One way to answer that question is to ask another. Why might I want to eat this every night? Perhaps this kind of eating comforts me in such a way that it allows me to escape all the other rigors of life. Perhaps this is how my family ate, and since I can't really go back to childhood, I use this as a way of feeling close to them. This issue is a bit clearer when we talk about outright addiction. So, for example, if I'm an alcoholic, I might say that I want a drink. But do I really want that drink, even though earlier today I swore I'd stop drinking? Or, am I just compelled to drink by the obsessive/compulsive disorder called addiction.

But compulsions are not just related to addictions, in fact, more often than not, we are moved by compulsion or compulsive wants. These are most often directed at objects that seem to help us to cope with life in some way. I want to overeat *because* eating compulsively comforts the savage beast inside of me that is longing for something else I cannot even imagine having. I want to under-eat *because* I will gain the respect and love of others if I am really thin. I want to get promoted up to the highest tier of my corporation, *because* if I become the CEO then I will finally be somebody.

It is often quite difficult for us to sort out the fine distinctions between an ego-state's compulsive wants and true desire. For example, suppose a new job opportunity opens up at my workplace, for which I am undoubtedly qualified. The minute I read about the opening, my fantasies start salivating. I can just see myself in this new position, with its prestige, and the extra income that will come with it. Then I start imagining that extra vacation time and all the ways that I can spend that money and I get all excited. If I stay right there, I am likely to apply for and get this job and I might say then that I'd attracted my desires.

But in this case, I never stopped to consider the actual tasks of the job. Suppose, for example, that the job comes with a lot of political infighting, tough decision-making and constant contact with people. Suppose that I'm genuinely an introverted person, who prefers a peaceful environment in which to focus on my creative endeavors. This new job offer looks very different now, doesn't it? But we live in a world in which power, prestige and money seem to be survival tools. So, even if I do stop to consider the job's tasks I may take it anyway, because I am compelled by what I consider to be survival.

We can all see how this might be confusing, if we stop to think about it. The problem is that we haven't really been taught to think about these things from the perspective of sorting out the distinctions between true desire and compelling want. Instead, we've been taught that there is a "right" way and a "wrong" way. We've been taught that we are to be responsible. We've been taught a good work ethic. So, we not only get desire mixed up with compelling wants, but we also get it mixed up with the "shoulds" of our lives.

Many of our inner conflicts amount to a struggle between compelling want and some obligation—forget about desire! And the reason we get obligation mixed up with compelling want is because we have a compelling want to do the "right" thing. That compelling want is based on an identity that defines us as people who do the "right" thing. So, we say we want to do the "right" thing, when what we really mean is that we can't imagine ourselves any other way. The "right" thing has become the safe thing, or even the only thing.

So, now we have compelling wants, shoulds and the compelling wants to operate out of the shoulds. And this is how we have managed our lives. But we haven't yet even come close to seeking true desire. So, what is true desire? True desire is that thing that we deeply desire when everything else is stripped away. If we absolutely could not have money, power, prestige, relationship, or anything else that we typically want, what would we want then? When everything else is emptied out of its power to compel, that is where we find true desire. But very often if we could empty all the rest of its power, we might be left wondering what in the world we do now.

When I teach workshops I often challenge participants, "If I could give you anything in the world right now, what would you ask for?" I get many who call out, "I want to win the lottery." "So, okay," I say, "let's say that you've won a lottery, of—oh, let's make it really big, fifty million dollars—what are you going to do with it?" I get all kinds of answers starting with paying off debts and ranging through helping the kids, taking care of parents, and all the way to buying an island in the Pacific. "So, okay," I say, "you have all of that now, so what have you gained?" Several will say, "happiness." Others say, "peace of mind." And I say, "Well, that's what you really wanted all along. The money was just the method you used to get there."

Silence. That's definitely *not* what they wanted to hear. "That fantasy was fun though, wasn't it? But what if I tell you that you can have that happiness and peace of mind right here, right now, with or without the money. Would you still want it?" The surprise of all surprises is that if we are really honest, most of us would question whether or not we really want that happiness or peace of mind at all, now that we know we don't have to have money to get it. We emptied money of its power, and then we didn't know what to do.

We've already noted that we live in a world in which we believe that money is how we protect ourselves from the demons of suffering. Because that is so much a part of our psychology, we find it hard to believe that we could really have happiness without it. Simultaneously, we fear that having to have money makes us evil people—based on old outworn traditional archetypes of money as evil. Basically then we are damned if we do, and damned if we don't. This tremendous dichotomous conflict makes money quite powerful in our imaginations, and in our realities. But if we could look at money as but a commodity of trade, then we have to ask what we are trading it for.

What do we want? Bottom-line. After everything else is said and done, what do we truly desire? In order to answer this question we have to make an inner journey. We have to go within to really ask what is the bottom-line for us. And then, once we've made that inner journey, we can begin to give ourselves our desires. That inner journey involves sorting. And the first thing we are going to have to decide about sorting is what we are sorting. Are we sorting between "wrong" and "right?" Are we sorting between having and not having? Are we sorting between our New Age/New Thought versions of ego and higher-self? Or, are we sorting finally between true desire and all of its close facsimiles.

It is extremely difficult for us to stop sorting between "wrong" and "right" because we were weaned on this philosophy that there is a "right" and a "wrong" and that if we want to be rewarded with a "good" life, we must be "good" people. Most of us know by now that "good" people often go unrewarded and "bad" people often get the rewards. But we don't want to cave in and become "bad" people, so we just keep perpetuating the old philosophy. We've touched on this idea in earlier chapters and will detail it in later chapters. But for now, all we need to know is that this duality thinking splits us off from awareness of our own souls. If then we identify ourselves as "good" people, a definition that is relative to the entire package of obligatory arrangements, then we are going to see ourselves as becoming better people, the more we forego the soul in honor of the obligation. And we are going feel that to stop sorting between the "good" and the "bad" and start sorting between true soul desire and obligation will make us into selfish, i.e., "bad" people.

If we sort between having and not having, on the other hand, we end up identifying our sense of ourselves with one or the other. Having generally equates with success and happiness and not having with failure or insignificance. If we identify with either of these, we believe that we *are* what we have. This becomes even more confusing when we attach morality to having and not having.

For instance, many of our religions teach that living without makes one holier, or closer to the Divine. Down through history in the Christian religion, many have taken a vow of poverty, thinking that this made them more accessible to Divine influence. Also, throughout history many Buddhists, Jainists, Hindis, Muslims, and others have become ascetics in order to avoid owning and being owned by things, property and any other aspect of the world. So, in our archetypal memory, we hold not having to be holier than having. And yet, we want to have. So, if we have in order to be successful and happy, does this make us "bad" people? If we do not have and see ourselves as failures, does this make us "good" people?

Finally, much of New Age/New Thought philosophy and the current understanding of the law of attraction actually blur our ability to see clearly our truest desires, because they tell us to split ourselves off between ego and higher self. The truth, however, is that if we are operating from true desire then ego has been absorbed into Self, not dismissed from it. So, operating from true desire would mean that I'm looking to unite the various aspects of myself rather than continue to compartmentalize them. This would mean that when my truest desires are manifest, I'm completely congruent.

So, suppose I learn that my truest desire is for peace. What now? I begin by looking within to my own internal resources for peace. We will explain this further in later chapters, but what I will find when I explore the inner terrain is that there is a place inside of me in which I already have peace. It's like an internal home for me, where peace and joy, the things I most desire on the earth plane, already exist on the soul plane. In fact, the only reason that I so desire these on the earth plane is because I already know them on a soul level.

Now that I have located my internal storehouse of peace, I might begin to look to my closest proximity for other matching energies. I might find that my partner and I have a deep camaraderie that matches my inner structure of peace. So, without effort, I can naturally allow and bring forth my own energy for the growth of that relationship. I might find that my home is symbolic for me of that inner home of peace and that, with or without knowing it, I have already created in the external world a home of peace that matches my internal peace. If, however, I find that either one of these close proximities is out of sync with my own authentic home, I can offer change energy to it.

This doesn't mean that if my relationship is really majorly out of sync with that inner structure, that I will get my partner to change to match it. But it does mean that I begin to recognize the difference and address it, by beginning to live out of my own internal home, rather than using the external as my source of life. This means that every encounter I have with my external world, including those with my partner, will *come from* my internal place of peace. I do not do this, however, *because* if I do then my partner will change and I can finally have peace. I do it as a natural outpouring of the peace I've found within. When we are talking about true desire, there are no *becauses*. *Becauses* bargain with life, whereas true desire brings Life to life, from the inside out.

With our current understanding of the law of attraction, we seem to be putting an awful lot of energy into the idea of attracting *from the external world* the things that we need. This goes completely against the grain of many of our deepest esoteric teachings, about which we will discuss a great deal more in a later chapter, in which the fountains of abundance come first from within. But if we first look within then all we need to do is be true to what we find there, and step-by-step we will create an external world that matches it.

Therefore, I won't need to nag and cajole my partner into coming around to my way of thinking. I will simply begin to live in my own inner home of peace and utilize the energy of that place to speak and act in ways that offer my external world a matching outer home. For example, if my partner is emotionally abusive, playing come here/go away games with my heart, my first job would be to realize how different this is from my own internal home. Then I will begin to speak and act in my external world just as my internal world bids. At some point this may or may not mean that I'll be urged from within to speak to my partner, requesting that he join me in that effort. If I do that and I'm coming from deepest desire rather than compulsion, my partner might feel and hear the sincerity and respond with equal sincerity. But then again, he may not. In fact, he might say, through words, actions or non-actions, "Well, I don't think I can give you that." In this event, I may need to leave the relationship, but I have restored peace in my external world because I am no longer on the roller coaster my partner and I built.

Of course, I could say, "But I can't have peace without my partner!" The truth is, however, that I didn't have peace *with* my partner either. And I absolutely can have peace, if I go within to find it and then carry it out into my world. If I choose to leave, it may mean a period of being single, while using this time to get to know myself. In getting to know myself, I may create all kinds of peaceful structures in my external life for which I would not have had energy if I'd stayed in the relationship.

But this is typically where it gets confusing, for I want the partner I have to be the one that I want—which essentially means I want him to be a different person or at least be living a different role. So, rather than take the risk to leave him because he cannot or will not match my peace energy, I might stay and demand that he change. And, if you ask me, I'll tell you that staying is my truest desire. So, I'll hammer and chisel away at him *because* this might make him change. This is compulsive want. It carries a *because.* I want him to change *because* if he changes then I can be happy with him. True desire recognizes that we already have peace; so, we don't need someone else to change so that we can have it. True desire simply wishes to manifest the internal world of peace in the external.

We can do this same kind of effortless work on every level of living, from parenting to jobs, friends and relationships with members of our families-of-origin. Of course, when parenting is the issue, leaving our children is not generally an option, though in some extreme circumstances it definitely can be a loving choice. But on every level, the same process applies. We recognize the internal place of peace and joy, start living from that place, and as we do, we simultaneously create that same peace and joy in the external world.

The current misconception of the law of attraction is that the external world is not what we need it to be because the ego has been running it. If we can get the ego out of the way and think only "positive" thoughts and feel only "positive" feelings, we can attract from the external world all kinds of wonderful things that will make us happy. The concept of true desire does not believe that anyone or anything outside of us can *make* us happy. Nor does it believe that we attract *from* the external world. Rather, we *give to* the external world, what we find deep within us, coming *from* the energy of that deep inner place. Further, true desire assimilates ego into the soul, rather than sending ego away. And true desire does not have to strive to think "positive" thoughts and feel "positive" feelings. Instead it simply goes deep within to find the Divine Self, and gives that to the external world. But, of course, this is all so very different from the myriad ways we've been taught to bargain with our lives.

4

Bargaining: a Stage of Acceptance

Acceptance is not a term we hear much when it comes to the law of attraction, because the term usually carries the connotation of settling. But as we shall see, acceptance is one of the basic tools we use in activating the law of attraction in our lives, for the art of acceptance is the very essence of reception. In order to *have* abundance, we must be able to *receive or accept* abundance. But acceptance is a process, and one that carries with it the exact same stages as the commonly known stages of grief, originated by Dr. Elisabeth Kübler-Ross in her famous book *On Death and Dying*—except, that I have changed her *depression* stage to the *sorrow* stage. Because we live in a dualistic world, anything that we are going to accept will process through, to one degree or another, the following stages: Denial, anger, sorrow, bargaining and finally acceptance. But we often get stuck in the bargaining stage, simply because it seems to offer a kind of illusory hope not offered by the other stages.

All of those *becauses* we learned about in the previous chapter were based in bargaining. In order to carry out a bargain there must be an IF and there must be a THEN. IF I give you this $2.99, THEN you will give me that loaf of bread. In the scenario presented in the previous chapter, we saw that I might stay in a relationship with a partner I think I can change *because* IF I can change him, THEN I can at last be happy without having to take any risks. In fact, our current understanding of the law of attraction is actually a bargain: IF I can control my thoughts, THEN I can have what I want. But this, like all other psychological bargains, actually blocks us from attaining our truest desires, simply because it is based in a bargain rather than in our deepest essential nature.

The fulfillment of our truest desires does not come about because we bargain with the external world, but rather because we find our needs and desires met within, and then we give that gift found inside to our external world. There is no IF, no THEN, and no *because.* Yet, much of our energy is literally stuck in the bargaining stage as we bargain with the realities of our lives, using all manner of fantasy, irrational beliefs and behavior patterns.

In order to fully understand the "stuck place" of bargaining, we must give several examples. So, let's start at the beginning. Parents bargain with parenting in several ways, depending on their particular ego-states or identities. In the following fictitious example, Sharon lives out of a Scapegoat identity, in which she feels responsible for the well-being of other people and is motivated by guilt to always serve and take care of others, so that she acts out that role in every area of her life, including in her parenting endeavors. But the fact is that even that very identity is a bargain she made many years ago when she was a child. Perhaps, she had parents who could not admit when they were wrong, did not nurture her and even felt burdened by her existence. She began to bargain with this reality. IF she could take on the burden of her own existence by feeling guilty for being alive and telling herself that she was responsible for their lacks, THEN they would need her, so that she would not have to worry that they would one day abandon her. And now IF she can assume that role with everyone, THEN she can be assured that they need her and won't ever leave.

Of course, people do leave over time, but she might just assume that this is because she didn't take good enough care of them. So, now she is a parent and she is making the same bargain with her children: IF I take responsibility for everything about my children, including their happiness, THEN they will need me, and I will always have my children in my life. As all children do, her children do need her and she will find that she intuitively knows exactly what to do for them, as she has been practicing knowing what people want before they ask for an entire lifetime.

What is likely to happen here, is that her children will grow up holding her accountable for their happiness, because, since she's always done it for them, they don't trust their own initiative to get the ball rolling in their lives. Sharon won't understand this response at all, because she's always had such great initiative, even initiating other people's projects. She has no idea that her bargain has also given her children a bargain: IF I can stay close to my mother and get her to take care of everything, THEN I'll be safe and loved all of my life. And that comes with another bargain: IF I can't find happiness, safety and love, THEN it is her fault.

We think that these bargains keep us safe from suffering. But in fact, they simply prolong our suffering. If Sharon had been provided a safe place from which to accept her parents as they were when she was a child, she might have allowed herself to experience the anger and sorrow that comes with the realization that they just didn't have the capacity to love and nurture her as she needed. Yet in that process of acceptance, she would have eventually realized that their lacks really didn't have to do with her worth or lovability at all, but rather with their own incapacity. But, like most of us, Sharon did not have the safety or the strength to accept that as a child, and at each stage of her life in which the possibility of accepting it was presented again, she had so adapted to the notion that she didn't have the safety or strength that she again refused to accept it. This made it scarier and scarier to actually allow such acceptance, so that by now, she has built a wall barring that acceptance. It will take a crisis bigger than the wall to help her to see. If the wall comes down, however temporarily, and she responds to that by getting some professional help or gains wisdom in some other way, she might just begin to connect the dots between the current crisis, and her old unresolved emotions. However, if she doesn't respond to this crisis with openness, she's likely to just ramp up the energy of the bargains. This will continue to happen again and again in her life until she either dies or she stops bargaining and moves to acceptance.

But it's fairly easy to see that if she ever does move to acceptance—realizing that her parents did not have the capacity to love her as she'd hoped and that she doesn't, therefore, have to continue to take on guilt and responsibility for others in an effort to vicariously get her parents to change—she's going to gain in strength and insight as a result of this process. She's going to find resources within herself that she did not know she had, because she's been so busy running from the facts of her early life. She may find a spiritual self, an emotional self, a psychological self she didn't know she had. She may learn to parent herself in all the ways her parents never could. She may find within new capacities for such things as unconditional love that she never expected to find.

We can see that resolving these life-long bargains makes a tremendous difference in how we are able after that to receive Life on Life's terms. And acceptance is the key to that ability to receive, for how will we receive something we cannot or do not accept? So, let's look at some of the other bargains we might make as parents.

Parenting Bargains

Letting go is one of the hardest of parental tasks, and yet the entirety of good parenting is based on a slow and loving letting go process that allows our children to learn to stand on their own two feet and step further and further out of our influence. We don't want to think about this as parents. We want to think that we are having little children who will always do as we wish them to do, who will grow up to be the people we imagine that they should be, and who will always favor our fragile ego-attachments to their lives, with tender, loving care. But in fact, our children are people in their own right, and have been from the moment they were born. They have nothing to do with our fragile ego-states and ego-attachments, and they are perfectly entitled to find themselves and their own life's goals and missions by taking up their own journeys.

It is not our right, nor is it our duty, to collude with our co-parents to mold our children into anything. They have an authentic Self when they get here. What they don't have when they get here is a split-off between conscious and unconscious realms of living. But from the moment of birth forward they are being challenged to interact with the world from something other than the authentic Self. What we teach them, when we try to mold them into some version of "child" that we would like them to be, is to split-off. It's as if they say, "Oh, my parents, who represent my survival, need me to be this or that. So, I'll be the person they want me to be and I'll repress who I really am." So, now the child has a conscious "me" and an unconscious "me," for this is the beginning of the split-off between the conscious and unconscious.

Many years ago, we would have called this a good thing, because the authentic "me" was considered to be made up of original sin. But a new thought has begun to take hold, in which we are beginning to recognize that the original "me" is the real deal. Still, there is yet enough of that old archetype hanging around to create considerable confusion about this issue. In addition, parents have most often come from homes in which the attempt was to mold them, at least to some degree, and so they believe in molding their children. Further, we don't want to just let our children run wild without any guidance whatsoever. So, as we evolve into the best and highest forms of parenting, we are going to have to solve the following riddle: How do we guide and discipline children while simultaneously allowing them to be true to their own authenticity? Most of us haven't even begun to grapple with that question, however, because at the same time that we are having and beginning to raise our children, we are also still bargaining with our own upbringing. And so we bargain with our children's lives as part of that package.

The reason it is so tempting to stay stuck in bargaining is that it always offers us a secondary gain. Secondary gain is an unconscious benefit we get from a bargain. Unlike a primary gain, such as getting paid to do a job, secondary gains are secret. We make these kinds of bargains under the tables of our lives, which means that we usually don't even know that we are making them. And because that is true, we rarely know why we have made them. In fact, they happen rather impulsively and compulsively, which means that we are driven by deep unsatisfied and usually unconscious needs to make them. But the unconscious need being met through the bargain is the secondary gain, the secret benefit we get from making our bargain. With regard to parenting, and since we are most often still bargaining with our own parents while we are raising our children, what generally happens is that our children are put into the bargaining equation in hopes that they will be able to vicariously satisfy some unmet childhood need of our own. Some examples follow.

When we parent using the *Overprotection Bargain*, the bargain and its accompanying secondary gain look like this: IF I can face Johnny's challenges for him, THEN he will need me, and THEN he won't ever leave me. Now if you ask Marie, Johnny's overprotector, what she is getting from overprotecting Johnny, she's usually going to tell you that she gets nothing from it, that it is hard to take care of all of his needs, and that she is only doing what any normal loving parent would do—keeping her child safe. But normal loving parents look at her behavior around Johnny and they are very clear that there is some major overprotecting going on. We can see then, that denial plays a role in the bargaining equation. What Marie doesn't want to know is that there is anything in this for her. She doesn't want to know that she is actually seeking something that her bargain promises to give her. She wants to see herself as a good parent. But in this fictionalized case, Marie actually has some old unresolved abandonment issues that she is attempting to resolve through Johnny. She can see no harm to Johnny in this, so there's a big unconscious shrug of the shoulders as she secretly says to herself that it is okay for her to hover over him, making all of his choices and overcoming all of his challenges. But in reality, Johnny is most probably not only going to feel smothered at some point, but he is not going to know, when he arrives at adulthood's door, how to manage normal life challenges. And even if he wants to break free of his mother, he'll probably engage in relationships only with people who will take care of him. And now that we understand bargaining a bit better, let's look at some other bargains.

The *Bully Bargain*: IF I can be "bigger and badder" than you, THEN you will never be "bigger and badder" than me, and I'll be safe. Safety is the secondary gain then, so that when the issue is parenting, the more the child "behaves" or complies with the bully parent, the more safety the bully feels. And, of course, children are the perfect victims because they are small and easily tricked. This bargain is easy to identify with because it offers the illusion of strength and is transferrable to almost any encounter—except those with people who appear to be "bigger and badder." The bargain is generally learned as a response to parents who either bully or consistently cave to the child's demands.

The *Respect Bargain*: IF I can get my children to respect me in certain definable ways, THEN I don't have to learn how to respect myself. Often I have worked with parents who insist that the only problem in their household is that their children don't respect them. Actually, however, the problem is that the parent is insisting that certain unrealistic expectations mean respect. So, if a child disagrees with the parent, he is not respecting the parent.

Or, if the child expresses anger at the parent appropriately then she is not respecting the parent. These bargains simply pass onto the child the unresolved issues of self-respect the parent brought to the dynamic. So, while the parent is secretly hoping the child can fix what was broken in the parent's childhood, the child is learning the same lack of self-respect.

The *Rigid-Discipline Bargain*: IF I can make my children walk the line, THEN I feel that I have control over whether or not they turn out as I think that they should, which, of course, will make me into a good parent. And the *Laissez Faire Bargain*: IF I let them do whatever they want, THEN they'll think I'm really a cool parent and they'll always love me. Either way, the child is the victim of the parent's unresolved issues. The *Manipulation Bargain*: IF I can manipulate them, THEN I will manage them without their knowing that I need to manage them.

Now we might look at some of these bargains and say, for example, well of course a child needs discipline, so we are going to have to bargain some and manipulate some to get them to behave. But this is a bargain in and of itself. It assumes that discipline is the same as control. And it denies the child's natural capacity as a sentient, albeit, immature being. Children don't respect or disrespect us because they are "good" or "bad" kids or because we haven't demanded their respect loud enough. They respect or disrespect us based on whether or not we have genuinely earned their respect. They don't obey or disobey us because we've done such a great job of punishing them or manipulating them. They obey or disobey us because that is the choice that makes the most sense to them at the time. Bargaining enables us to lie to ourselves about the capacities of our children.

Acceptance, on the other hand, helps us to come to terms with the fact they, like us, have the capacity for choice. It allows us to recognize our children's ability to choose and help them to use choice consciously and with some regard for their own and others' well-being. This means that we can make room for that capacity as we are parenting. So, if the child has a tendency to act up in the toy department of the store, the parent might say something like: "You have a choice about what you will do here. So, if you choose to behave according to the rules we've discussed, you are also choosing to go to the park after we leave the store. But if you choose to disregard those rules, then you are choosing not go to the park." Dependent on the age of the child, the choices can grow in responsibility—which ultimately teaches the child how to manage life in the adult world. Now, many would say that such an arrangement gives the child the option to misbehave and so we should spank them or threaten to spank them for better results. But, again, we deny reality when we assume that any particular methodology forces a child to behave. The child has a choice—whether we admit that to ourselves or not.

However, this fact of choice does not mean that children don't *feel* forced sometimes, nor does it say that we should blame a child for an adult's manipulative efforts. For example, if a child is sexually abused by a manipulative parent, she usually wants very badly to believe that her abuser is good and kind and would never do anything to harm her. Thus, she is easier to trick. So, though there is some limited choice involved, it is not the choice of an adult, it is not informed choice, nor is it choice that can be considered to be anything more than choosing to go unconscious so that one does not have to realize what is happening.

So, I am not saying here that children have the wisdom, maturity or strength of adults and can make adult choices. What I am saying is that children make choices within the capacity of their own childlike and childish reasoning. There are many choices that our children make every day. Like whether or not to clean up their rooms, or whether or not to pick up that fork and toddle toward the power outlet with it, or whether or not to say "no" to a certain directive, or whether or not to try that first hit of ecstasy. How we respond to each of these and other choices sets up an interactive pattern between parent and child, that allows children to respond to a series of parental choices with a series of life-altering choices of their own.

Parents simply cannot remove the fact of choice from a child's life. What this means is that whipping a child does not force the child into compliance. The child may choose to act out less because he fears the punishment, but he is still choosing. In fact, such punishment quite often offers the child an opportunity to experiment with a boundary question: If I act worse, will they hit me harder or longer? Those of us who work in the mental health field have seen many examples of kids who, though physically punished strictly, continued to act out in more and more difficult-to-control ways. Mike, one fictitious example, does this because he carries a bad-kid identity. Like a ghost who can move matter, Mike came to understand on some level that he could get his parents to see him by acting a certain way. A long series of actions and reactions have helped him to come to this magical-thinking conclusion. It's as if he is thinking, "Wow! I exist now. I can tell that I exist when my parents get really mad and slap me around!" His heart may be broken by the fact that they don't seem to notice him unless he is acting out, but he has no one and no resources to deal with such enormous sorrow. So, he bargains with anger instead. And since he has no one to help him with that either, he just acts out. It is as if his actions were saying, "Why did you have me if you didn't even want to be bothered with me?" And so he bargains with existence by developing the bad-kid identity.

This series of choices with which Mike has identified may not be conscious, informed or adult choices, but they are, nevertheless, choices. And they are life-altering choices because they can change the path of the life from one of authenticity, to one in which the child lives bound to a mask, costume and role for many years.

Life Bargains

Life bargains are bargains with authenticity. Instead of living from the authentic Self, we bargain with life energy and creativity by pretending. So it is that these bargains altar both the identity and the life path. Some examples:

The Good-Guy Bargain: IF I can always try to be very good, THEN I don't have to feel like the bad person I suspect I am.

The Invisible Man Bargain: IF no one has ever really noticed me, THEN I may assume that noticing me is wrong, or even dangerous. Therefore, IF I stay invisible, THEN I don't ever have to be afraid of myself.

The Scapegoat Bargain: IF I can manage my life by guilt, by taking responsibility for others and by sacrificing my authenticity for them, THEN they will need me and stay, AND I'll feel that my life's mission is very noble.

The Runaway Bargain: IF I can run from every sticky emotion or situation, THEN I don't have to deal with any difficulties in life.

The Fixed-Position Bargain: IF I can just find my position and not move, THEN I don't ever have to be afraid of uncertainty.

The Big Baby Bargain: IF I can get you to take care of my every need, THEN I won't ever have to learn to take care of myself. Besides, it makes you feel good, doesn't it?

The Blame Bargain: IF I can always keep my finger pointed away from me, THEN I don't ever have to take the risk to take responsibility for my own choices or the even greater risk of getting to know myself.

> The Chaos Bargain: IF I can keep many plates spinning, IF I can start fires, IF I can raise the ante, THEN everything is so blurry that I don't really have to take responsibility for making good decisions.
>
> The Superwoman/man Bargain: IF I can be strong, fast, dependable, certain, and capable in all ways, at all times, THEN I don't ever have to feel sad or afraid about all of the ways that I am consistently let down by others.
>
> The Control Bargain: IF I can delude myself into believing that I'm always in control, THEN I don't have to deal with my intense fear of uncertainty.
>
> The Victim Bargain: IF I believe that life is way bigger than me, THEN I'm truly the victim of life and THEN I don't really have to be responsible for making choices that would make my life better.
>
> The Rescue Bargain: IF I can put all of my energy into fixing your life, THEN I don't have to take responsibility for fixing mine.

These bargains basically set us up with a life-plan. In fact, we can identify with these bargains in such a way that we come to believe they define us. People who consistently use the Control Bargain, for example, tend to develop the Bully identity. Whether they use manipulation, guilt, mind games, emotional, physical, verbal or sexual abuse; the bottom line is that they must be in control in order to stave off the fear of uncertainty about something. People who consistently use the Chaos Bargain or the Victim Bargain tend to develop the Victim identity. Ultimately the name of the game for both bargains is to avoid having to take responsibility for life. To learn more about these identities or roles please read *Restoring My Soul: A Workbook for Finding and Living the Authentic Self.*

Each of these bargains allows the person to fit into a particular mold, from which they can say, with a helpless shrug, "That's just me; what are you going to do?" In so doing, they believe that they are keeping themselves alive and safe. But actually they are simply giving themselves permission to stay stuck, doing the same old thing. These are hard patterns to break simply because they have become identity. Because that is so, we tend to stay stuck until the patterns are broken by a crisis so big that we cannot help questioning the nature of the identity. Each of these bargains carries with it a mantra of self-talk that allows us to continually talk ourselves into doing what we have always done. For example, the mantra of the Runaway Bargain might be, "Get over it!" because if she can tell herself or others to just get over it, then she doesn't have to be present for a single difficult issue. For the Victim, the mantra might be "I can't," "I had no choice," or "you just don't understand how hard it is," so that there is always a silent or overt demand for someone else to take care of him.

Career Bargains

And the Life Bargains we make very often carry us into careers or jobs in which we make even more bargains. The following fall into that category.

> The Money-Maker Bargain: IF I can have money, THEN I don't need to worry about whether or not I like or am a good match for this job; just give me the money and I'll get everything I need from that.

> The Proving Myself Bargain: IF I can be tough and strong and just suck it up, THEN I will have shown all those people who thought I didn't have it, AND I won't have to take responsibility for my own happiness.

The Provider Bargain: IF I am a good provider for my family, THEN I am a good person. Nothing else matters.

This-Is-As-Good-As-It-Gets: IF this is as good as it gets, THEN I don't have to take responsibility for my own goals in life.

The Everyone Else/No One Else Bargain: IF no one else I know has a job that makes him happy, THEN I don't have to do that either. And IF everyone else has to work to survive, THEN how do I think that I have the right or privilege to work from the love and joy that is within me?

The Making-it Bargain: IF I can achieve the prestige, money or power that I need, THEN I have made it, and I don't have to look any deeper for my unresolved respect issues and power needs.

The Comparison Bargain: IF I am busy measuring myself by what I perceive others have, THEN I don't have to really take responsibility for finding out what I desire and living into it.

With these bargains we see both subtle and overt refusals to take responsibility for our own happiness. As adults we pretty much get four realms of endeavor in which we can live into our truest natures: Self, relationship, parenting and career. Career takes up anywhere from forty to sixty hours of a given week, in which there are, depending on our sleep patterns, a little over one hundred hours of awake time in a seven-day week. Some higher level executives, professionals or independent entrepreneurs consistently work eighty hours a week. Where then is the time for the other three areas of life? Even if we don't work that hard, we spend much of our time in the career realm. And if that time is spent bargaining with our happiness, then we have impacted the entire life energy.

We have been taught both subtly and overtly that work is a survival tool. It is what puts food on the table and we believe that's what it's meant to do. Additionally, we have an archetypal belief that without work, we will not survive, so we have a broad fear-base from which we operate within the career realm. On top of that, we have the above bargains, which we can see now, clearly demonstrate our resistance to doing what we love. We even hear our current movie idols saying things like "And they pay me to do this!" in utter surprise that they have the privilege of doing what they love.

Though many of us are thinking a bit differently now, we still struggle with our own archetypal fears in this area. Our current understanding of the law of attraction tells us that if we want a better career, then we should start imagining ourselves in the career of our dreams, create a vision board, do affirmations and go back to school or start looking for the job we want, for in so doing we will magnetize it. However, the understanding of the law of attraction discussed in this book asserts that it runs much deeper than magnetizing an external to make the internal happy. Rather, we might need to look at the various bargains we are making with career, find out what the secondary gain is for us and see if there is a way to meet that secondary gain more directly—and perhaps in a different area of endeavor. So, if we are seeking to resolve unresolved issues about personal respect, for example, we might need to go more directly to *personal* respect rather than trying to get it by bargaining for *professional* prestige and power.

Unresolved issues are unresolved because they have been sent away into the unconscious, through all of our various attempts at bargaining. But our issues have a message for us, a message meant to be heard, really heard for exactly what they are saying. And the unresolved issue cries out to be embraced and brought home to live as a vulnerable and hungry child would live in the home of a great, wise and loving king.

Relationship Bargains

The truth is that for centuries, with but a few rare exceptions, we've been engaging in relationships without learning the essential skills that would build an authentic, intimate connection with an equal partner. Below are some of the bargains that have kept us from developing those skills.

The Come Here/Go Away Bargain: IF I can get you to stay and be my yo-yo, THEN I can have relationship without having to take the risk to be intimate.

The Commitment Phobia Bargain: IF I can avoid commitment, THEN I don't ever have to be intimate with anyone, which means I won't have to take the risk that they will reject me as they get to know me.

The Enmeshment Bargain: IF I don't do what they want, THEN they will reject me. IF I don't agree with them or IF I have a different personality from theirs THEN I am somehow betraying them. Therefore, IF I conform, THEN I don't ever have to take the risk to be free to be me.

The Detachment Bargain: IF I can keep you at a safe distance, THEN I don't ever have to worry that you'll get close enough to hurt me.

The Possessive Bargain: IF you belong solely to me, THEN I don't have to worry about whether or not I belong solely to me.

The Triangulation Bargain: IF we can keep a third party between us, such as money, children, time, in-laws, gossip, THEN we don't really have to be intimate.

The Cheating Bargain: IF I can keep one foot in one relationship and one foot in another, THEN I can experiment with one without losing the other, AND I don't have to be intimate with either.

The Bridge-Builder Bargain: IF I can build bridges over all the gaps in our relationship, THEN neither you nor I will ever really know there *are* gaps in our relationship; AND I won't ever really have to wonder whether or not you would have built your half of the bridge if I hadn't done it for you.

The Abuse Bargain: IF I have absolute power over you, THEN I'm assured you belong to me, and only if you belong to me can I assure myself that I'm okay.

The Sex Bargain: IF we are good in bed, THEN that's as far as we need to go to make this relationship intimate. Or, IF I can have sex with lots of people, THEN I don't have to do the work and take the risks of intimacy, AND I can convince myself that I'm not really lonely. Or, IF I can perform well in bed, THEN I am an okay person.

The Trust = Love Bargain: IF I decide to trust you simply because I love you, THEN I don't have to take the risk to find out if you are able to earn my trust.

The Security Bargain: IF I can just get married and settle down, THEN I am financially and emotionally secure, and that's really all that matters.

We can clearly see that many of these secondary gains have to do with an avoidance of intimacy. Intimacy is one of the hardest things we do in any relationship, because intimacy is all about deep and meaningful self-revelation. We are so used to lying, covering up, hiding and pretending that when we get into a relationship, we very often feel that we got there because we lied, covered up, hid and pretended really well. Somewhere deep down inside there's a mantra saying, "If they really knew me, they wouldn't stay."

Why is that mantra there? It's not because of low self-esteem, though we can certainly have low self-esteem in this dynamic as well. Rather, it is because our very first bargain was based on this premise. The reason we first split-off into conscious and unconscious realms is because we wanted to hide our authenticity from parents we knew would reject it if it was exposed to them. And we've been hiding it ever since. The fear of our parents' abandonment was so huge, that we literally split ourselves in half to compensate for it. Some of our parents would definitely have done it differently if they'd only known that all they needed was a mirror for us to look into, unfiltered by their agendas. Some of them would not have done it differently, even if they'd known. But, now, we've grown to fear intimacy greatly.

The other thing that we can clearly see in the secondary gains is that we also have a fear of owning and taking responsibility for ourselves. Not only do we not wish to be known by others, but we also fear that if we know ourselves we will somehow be betraying the ethic in which we were raised. That ethic mostly gave us a double message. Verbally many of us got, "Just be yourself." But behaviorally, what we got was, "Don't you dare be yourself. Be who we need you to be!"

So, the self we allow ourselves to be is the one that was most agreeable to our parents, stuck in their own bargains. Actually, that "self" was a role we played. And even if that role was extremely difficult and quite distorted—it was better than taking the risk of losing whatever little piece of security that role gave us. The self that our partners want and need to know, however, is the authentic Self. In a healthy committed primary relationship we are going to need to build intimacy. Intimacy requires authenticity. Two people who are not authentic are not likely to establish intimacy, because intimacy means self-revelation—and how will we reveal a self we don't even know? But of course, intimacy can help us to become aware of our authenticity, for the more we reveal of ourselves to a significant other, the more we come to know both our internal conflicts, which can lead us to our deeper resonating potency. Of course, there is still the silent work one does alone, which adds yet more to intimacy, but real relationship is made of real relating. Instead, most of the time, two roles are attracted to each other because they prop each other up—a dynamic we will learn much more about in the following chapter—a dynamic made up entirely of relationship bargains.

Relationship bargains, like all other bargains, are agreed upon under the table. We don't agree on these things out in the open, for if we did the secondary gains we could achieve with these bargains would be diminished. For example, if I'm using the Sex Bargain so that what I want to do is just have sex but not really get intimate, then I'm not likely to say that out loud, because to do so is a form of intimacy. But if I do mention that I'm just in it for sex, then I'm not likely to say, "Listen I only want sex here, because intimacy scares the Be-Jesus out of me, because I was afraid my parents would abandon me if I were true to myself." Or, "Listen, I'm really lonely, but I don't want anyone to know me, so my solution to that problem is to just have sex with lots of people." These confessions of the inner world's conflicts would undermine the potential secondary gain of not having to be known, would they not? No, these are deals made with a silent, unspoken handshake. These are deals that we don't want to know we are making.

And the biggest deal about these deals is that they keep us further out of touch with our personal power and a very natural and deeply-rooted internal home, within which we can find true peace and joy. Without a strong connection and easy access to this place, we are bargaining with the energy of life itself and in so doing misusing the power of the *true* law of attraction.

As we said in the previous chapter, we don't attract from the outer world to the inner. Nothing out there can make us happy and fulfilled—not even our partners. We go within to this deep inner home and find there our own peace and joy and then we give that peace and joy to our outer worlds. But these relationship bargains are based on the assumption that our partners either make or break us, and so we have to wheel and deal to work with it. For example, if I am using the Trust = Love Bargain, trusting you simply because I love you, not because my intuition and that deep home within agree with what I see in you; then I am avoiding contact with that deep home and my own intuition in order to hold on to you.

Trust comes from within to without, the same way the law of attraction works. My intuition in accompaniment with my emotional responses to your behavior and words, as well as my physical responses to your presence will all tell me whether or not I can trust you. If I am solely looking outside of myself, asking that you inform me as to whether or not I can trust you, then I am asking that you convince me that you are right for me. If your intuition picks up on my unspoken request, then you are going to do everything you think that I need you to do, in order to stay involved with me. One day, perhaps after I have awakened to the seriousness of my wounds, the mask and costume will fall off. When it does, I'm likely to say, "I don't even know who you are." And I'll be right. But the reason I don't know you is because we made a deal under the table. We both agreed that you would put on a mask and costume that looked, walked, talked, acted, spoke and in every way pretended to be all that I wanted you to be, so that I could trust you. And that deal looked like a far better deal to me than the one in which I would take responsibility for myself by looking within to find out what is true for me there, and perhaps as a result, removing myself from this relationship before it hurt.

If I want to attract a healthy relationship then, my first step in that process is going to be a steady and wide-eyed gaze within, so that I can first see who I am, who I really am at the home base of me. And I'll need to learn how to live from that place, so that I can give what I find there back to my world in the form of a relationship. The same is true of any other of our bargains, be they parenting bargains, career bargains, or the basic life-bargains we mentioned earlier. And in order to do the work of going within, we are going to need to know what to look for in there. But we are often blocking awareness of what is going on in there with some bargains with mood.

Mood Bargains

When we are in a mood our thoughts, our behavior and our emotions are dominated by the mood. A mood can last anywhere from a few hours to several months. Because of the life bargains we make, we often suffer numerous setbacks and defeats until we finally settle into a place in which we try to cope by bargaining through mood. Or, we may have learned early to fold these mood bargains into our identities, because they worked so well to get us the secondary gains we were after. Here are some of the mood bargains.

The Pollyanna Bargain: IF I don't look, THEN I won't see. IF I don't see, THEN I'll feel no pain.

The Emotional Fatigue Bargain: IF I take on the emotions and problems of others, THEN I won't have to take responsibility for my own. I'm just too tired for that, and besides I don't have time for me; there's just so much of you.

The Chip-on-the-Shoulder Bargain: IF I can keep my guard up, ready always to duke it out with the unfairness of life, THEN I won't ever be hurt by life again.

> The Anxiety Bargain: IF I worry, THEN I'll at least be doing *something* about things over which I have no control. THEN I can tell myself that I have some measure of control.
>
> The Depression Bargain: IF I repress my emotional responses to life's challenges, THEN I won't have to feel them. This may take enormous emotional energy so that eventually I must make another bargain: IF I can give up my sense of self-worth, my interests and my happiness, THEN I won't have to take the risk to ask life for anything, and THEN I'll have outwitted further disappointment.

These bargains pretty much speak for themselves, but the main thing we need to remember about these moods is that they are meant to help us bargain with life on planet earth where people can suffer, and seemingly random problems and crises can occur. This means that these bargains in some way enable us to deal, however ineffectively, with that reality. For example, it is extremely difficult for persons who are very anxious to acknowledge the reality that there is much about life that cannot be controlled. That idea creates even more anxiety than does worrying. So, they worry as a way of telling themselves that they actually do have control. They are using energy and this makes them feel as if they are doing something. But the something they are doing is a bit like a rat running a maze over and over and never finding the cheese.

We must be very clear, however, when we are talking about mood bargains, for I am not saying that some people might not also need to be medicated when these mood bargains turn into mood disorders. Perhaps some have identified with a generational issue with bargaining, or perhaps there is a genetic component. Research has not yet concluded which came first, the chicken or the egg, for there is yet to be a conclusion to the nature/nurture argument. But there are many potentially effective treatments for these disorders. Yet where medication is a chosen treatment, regardless of whether it is taken for a lifetime or a period of time, it is best used as a platform from which we can do the work of building the rest of our lives.

That said, these bargains somehow acknowledge that life is way bigger than our power to live it effectively and are, for that reason, made up of magical thinking. If life were not the big, bad enemy, we would not need magical thinking to compensate for its power. The Depression Bargain, for example, assures us at its most fundamental level that we don't have to take ourselves and our desires seriously, by getting up out of the bed and finding the Self and the life we desire. Instead, we can just sit this one out. As I treat clients who are depressed, the most important determinant as to whether or not they will get beyond their depression is their willingness to utilize some desire to have a meaningful life to empower their ability to begin to take responsibility for meeting their own needs and fulfilling their own truest desires. Of course, this is a process, but those who do the work quite often get beyond their depression and come to later see the depression as the door through which they walked to find themselves. The other option, of course, is to continue to use these bargains to trade away invaluable treasures of the soul in order to maintain the mood.

The Pollyanna Bargain does just that but, unlike depression and anxiety bargains, it keeps us from having to consider suffering as a viable option at all. Sometimes I think that the current New Age understanding of the law of attraction is trying to get us all to make a Pollyanna Bargain. That understanding tells us that the world is illusion, that there is no suffering and that we should turn off the TV and radio and only listen to and watch those things that cause us to think "positive" thoughts. The interesting thing about this instruction is that the reason we are to do this is *so that we will not suffer* the backlash of "negative" energy that comes from thinking "negative" thoughts. But if there is no suffering, then why are we so worried about suffering? So, like the Pollyanna Bargain, we tell ourselves to think only "positive" thoughts and all the "bad" stuff will go away.

The idea that the world is illusion came about as a result of some misperceptions about what is meant by the language used in *A Course in Miracles.* The *Course* teaches that our perceptions of ourselves as less than Divine mean that we misperceive reality. This misperception "leads to a world of illusion, a world which needs constant defense precisely because it is not real" (Schucman 2007, x). Statements like these were taken out of context and literalized when they were translated to mean that the world is not real. In fact, what these very wise teachings intended to give us was a look at our inner worlds in which we wear the colored glasses of perception, so that we *perceive* an unreal world, an illusion of the world, based on the fact that we see ourselves as less than Divine. This invalidates our perceptions, ***not*** our world, so that once we recognize our own Divine nature, our perception of the world changes. Interpreting this beautiful lesson in literal terms means that we are creating a basis for many other erroneous spiritual concepts. These erroneous concepts have led many to now feel that to see the world as reality is to betray the basis of the entire New Age movement. But the author tells us that the *Course* "…is not intended to become the basis for another cult. Its only purpose is to provide a way in which some people will be able to find *their own Internal Teacher*" (viii, *emphasis added*).

Helen Schucman, the book's author, tells us that she received the information for *A Course in Miracles* first and later received the information for the Student Workbook (viii). But this student workbook institutes practices that have led to a great deal of misunderstanding about what the original book was trying to say. For example, in Lesson 14, we read this:

> With eyes closed, think of all the horrors in the world that cross your mind. Name each one as it occurs to you and then deny its reality.... Say for example: God did not create the war, so it is not real. God did not create that airplane crash, and so it is not real. God did not create that disaster (specify) and so it is not real (705)

What many students of the Workbook are getting from this is that we live in an unreal world. That there is a split-off between the things God made and the things God didn't make, and those that God didn't make are not real. But in the Introduction of the original Course, we read this:

> This course can therefore be summed up very simply in this way:
>
> [2]Nothing real can be threatened.
>
> [3]Nothing unreal exists.
>
> [4]Herein lies the peace of God (1).

The *Course* is trying to teach this one central lesson. This means that we have, attributed all manner of meaning to things, events, people, places and circumstances, based on the misperception that we are less than Divine. But the truth is that all is Divine, and therein lies the peace of God. Yet when we take literally the statement from Lesson 14 above, by denying the experiences of our lives, we only further perpetuate our problems.

So, if we take that statement literally, the plane crash didn't really happen. Now, I don't know exactly what Schucman meant when she wrote that statement, but I do know that the plane crash really did happen. Thousands of people really did transition out of this physical realm of existence on 9/11. The Trade Towers really did collapse. And we all had some kind of experience relative to that event.

But that event was created by all of us collectively, based on our misperception of ourselves as less than Divine Beings. How do we interpret that event? Does it mean that we are doomed to repeat such atrocities? Does it mean that we are "evil" people who will eventually collapse our world? Or, could it possibly mean that because we have all agreed to bargain with our own souls, so that we are blind to what is really going on, we created this potential together? Could it also mean, because our souls are still actively influencing all things, that somehow this tragedy will enable us to find ourselves at a deeper, more meaningful level? Could it also mean that all of those people who were killed that day did not really die, because no one dies? Answering these questions helps us to move beyond our own illusions about life and into the truth of our Divine nature.

So, when we talk about the world as illusion, we are telling ourselves that the happy little world we've created in our minds is the only reality. This is the very definition of the Pollyanna Bargain. While we may change our moods with this bargain, we are repressing many other emotions and thoughts in the process, and as we've seen this only builds more shadow material for us to have to deal with later. Further, how literally we take this idea that the world is illusion could actually create some very difficult mental health issues for some people.

The notion that the world is an illusion, when taken to its literal end, means that there is no material reality at all. If we were truly meant to believe that, then why were we given bodies and planted on the physical plane in the first place? Did the Divine make a mistake? "Oops, meant to create immaterial reality! Oh well, guess you'll have to live with it now. But here's the thing, IF you can convince yourselves that it doesn't really exist, THEN you'll be happy."

That was made deliberately humorous to make the point that we were planted in material reality for a reason. What if that reason is creativity itself? What if the slow progressive process of evolution out of the duality state and into an awareness of

Oneness and Beingness allows us to bring material reality into its finest material essence, because we live it as energy? What if material reality *is* the Divine in form? What if our journey here is to help us to come to terms with a corporeal existence *as* Divine Beings, because we are a part of the creative endeavor of the Divine, who has decided to combine form with formlessness? After all, nothing unreal exists. And nothing real can be threatened.

If we really believe that, then we know that it is our *fear of living* that is the problem, not the reality of the world. And it is our fear of living that pushes us to make bargains with life, with relationship, with parenting, with career and finally with mood in order to compensate for our fear. But if there is really nothing to fear then perhaps we could get on with creating the world of matter that is fully *ensouled*—fully aware of the soul within which it abides. Personally, I like the exercise in *A Course in Miracles Workbook for Students,* in which the author challenges the readers to make real the inherent Divine energy in the surrounding physical objects:

> First, close your eyes and repeat the idea for today several times, slowly. [2]Then open your eyes and look quite slowly about you, applying the idea specifically to whatever you note in your casual survey. [3]Say, for example:
>
> [4] *My holiness envelops that rug.*
> [5] *My holiness envelops that wall.*
> [6] *My holiness envelops these fingers.*
> [7] *My holiness envelops that chair.*
> [8] *My holiness envelops that body.*
> [9] *My holiness envelops this pen* (737).

This would be more like acceptance. When we accept the reality of who we are as Divine Beings, then we begin to use our powerful energies to overturn the tables in the temple, to stop the bargaining we are doing every day as we walk on sacred ground unawares. This is why acceptance is so very important. Acceptance is reception. Reception means that we receive what is.

Our current law of attraction has us basically rejecting reality in favor of something else that we've imagined would be better. So, if we have a "negative" thought or a difficult emotion we are to get rid of those so that they will not interfere with the world we are imagining. In fact, we are taught to imagine ourselves in the world of our dreams for a period of time at least twice a day, and then spend the rest of our days in gratitude for the life we now have. There's a lot of work involved in these activities and a lot of repression.

So, what if we are not really grateful for some aspect of life? Well, then we just have to keep affirming that we are grateful until we become grateful. What this amounts to is a repression of ingratitude in favor of a better emotion. Acceptance, on the other hand, allows us to receive ingratitude as a pathway to authenticity. Acceptance embraces that ingratitude, sitting down beside it to hear what it has to say. It asks that ingratitude explain itself and give us information about its source. The soul is sitting down to have a conversation with the mind. The mind is much more likely to be impressed with the power of soul energy, listening attentively to it, than it would be impressed with another mind activity simply discounting and repressing it. Once the soul has heard all that ingratitude has to say, it can then envelop ingratitude in its peaceful arms, utilizing the energy *behind* the ingratitude to bring mind and soul together in harmonious union.

What healthy acceptance looks like can be seen from the following fictitious example. Alyson is the adult child of alcoholic parents, who has grown up to marry an alcoholic husband. Further, she comes from a poor economic background in which she, not her parents, was the primary worrier and provider of sustenance. She and her husband now both have blue collar jobs but her husband gets fired quite frequently due to absenteeism. During his many stints of unemployment, she does what she's always done—she takes on two jobs. She does all of the housekeeping, grocery shopping and cooking, just as she did when she was a child and she bridges all of the gaps in their relationship by starting all the conversations, noticing and fixing all of the problems and generally taking care of everything. She may nag him to do his part, but deep down she knows that she's carrying the load and that if she doesn't do it, it simply won't get done.

Alyson is a very unhappy and resentful person, but she wears a happy face most of the time. She never tells her friends at work what is going on at home, but is there to listen to and advise them when they need a sounding board. In fact, looking at Alyson from the outside, no one would ever know how alone and burdened she feels most of the time. Alyson believes that if she just keeps a good attitude and is patient, things will eventually work themselves out. The problem with this belief is that it is the one she has had and been operating out of for her entire life. She has never stopped to ask herself if it is working for her, because if she does she might get a bad attitude.

But one day, either due to a crisis, or to a sudden awareness that comes about as a response to a slow, steady drip effect, Alyson realizes the enormity of her pain. It feels to her like a crushing blow of impossible proportions. But it is not impossible, for she is feeling it. Her pain drives her, as pain often does, to begin to ask herself some questions about her life, the quality of it, and the things that she might be missing out on as a result of the choices she's made to repeat her pattern.

One day Alyson decides to break down and tell a few of her friends how difficult her life is and how sad and troubled she is about it. They tell her that they've just gotten into this new literature about the law of attraction, informing her that all she needs to do is stop thinking "negative" thoughts and stop feeling "negative" feelings and spend some time every day meditating on positive affirmations about what she really wants. This advice feels to Alyson a lot like what she's already been doing, so she decides instead that she is going to go with the feelings she's having and just listen to them, because she senses that they have something to tell her. So, rather than meditating on what she would like in her life, for a time she meditates on what she is feeling as she examines the life she has lived thus far.

She opens up to her feelings, allowing herself to write them down so that she can clearly hear what they are saying. She spends considerable time in self-reflection, even as she is going through the routine of her days. She acknowledges that most of her life she has been afraid of anything that is different from the way she was raised. She begins to understand that she took on far more than most children have to take on and that she identified with her role, thinking that this was not only as good as it was ever going to get, but that hers was the only possible role she could ever play. She also begins to realize that she's been carrying a huge but hidden burden of sorrow most of her life, in which some part of her has always known that she longed for more love, nurturance and guidance from her parents than they were ever able to give. As she awakens to that truth, she begins to realize that she's been longing for that same love, nurturance and guidance from her husband and that he, too, was unable to give it. She sees that every single choice that she has made in her life to date has been a choice to continue to take care of people who would not care for her.

Now, if she stops right there all that will be known is that life is hard and somehow she's been picked out to have this hard life. But if she continues with the acceptance process, she will eventually have to conclude that *she* is now responsible for the choices she makes from this day forward. If she receives that information, allowing it to seep down into the deepest recesses of her psyche, bones and cells, then she can actually realize this as a unique opportunity to start giving herself all that love, nurturance and guidance she's never received from anyone else before.

If she's really listening, she knows that loving herself will mean loving every aspect of herself, including her own blind spots, her own misgivings, lack of confidence, low self-esteem and even her anger at her parents and her husband. Loving herself will not mean picking and choosing from among the different aspects of herself, which ones she will accept for love, and which she will reject. That's what she's been doing all along. Loving herself will mean taking that anger she finds within, sitting it on her lap as she would a little child and listening to what it says. That anger is telling her something about what she really needs. If she doesn't listen to it, she will not fully know what she needs.

As she slowly walks through the darkness of these so-called "negative" feelings, she receives more and more of herself, which had previously been lost to repression. Each feeling she has, whether so-called "positive" or so-called "negative, has power within it to give her back the loving gift of herself as she listens to its deeper meaning. One day she will go to her husband and say that she is done, that she must leave him because he is just not able to do his part in the relationship. He will balk and blame and cajole, but because of the clear boundaries created by her anger, she will be able to stand firm. The other voices within her that say she should stay and try to fix him, or stay and get him some help, or stay and make sure he doesn't kill himself will be seen for what they are—bargains with reality. She's already tried these things and has, by now, become clear that not only do they not work, but they are based on the illusion that she can do his job of living for him. Because she has listened to her feelings, she is able to clearly see that if she is 100% responsible for her life, he is likewise 100% responsible for his.

Once she leaves him, she is now free to consider the other areas of her life, such as her job, and ask herself some serious questions. What parts of her job does she like, and what does this tell her about her interests and talents? What parts does she dislike or even hate, and what does this tell her about her interests and talents? In this process, she is taking back parts of herself that she had long ago dismissed as unnecessary and even cumbersome. As she does this, she is beginning to get a taste for what kinds of things really intrigue and excite her. Once she gets a taste for that, she wants more and more of it.

Now Alyson is beginning to create a life that meets her truest desires. Each step she makes into her psyche is a step that much closer to her authentic Self. As she gains more and more of a perspective on life from that internal angle, she is learning more and more about her joy, her peace and the potent, passionate energy that generates everything else real in life—the soul. Alyson is becoming real. How is she doing this? She is receiving her own soul through the process of acceptance. And how will we manifest soul desires, without a relationship, a living, vibrant relationship with the soul? How will we live into our lives, in the fullest aspect that Life can present, without Living in the soul that is Life itself?

5

ID or I AM

When we come here, fresh from the other side and whatever life we lived prior to that, we are not empty. Before we actually take that first breath, we know ourselves at the soul level. But on the physical plane, where duality reigns, we look to our environment to give us an identity—an ID. We look to the faces and the body language of the people who change our diapers. We look to the body sensations we feel when we are wrapped in the arms of our primary caregivers. We look to the unresolved emotions floating in the air. We look to the looks given, the tones of voice and the touches to tell us who we are.

So, when an infant is approximately two months old, she can quite often be found staring at her own fist, as she begins to recognize it as a part of the body into which she's incarnated. "Oh," she might be heard thinking, "This hand is me." Not too much later, she opens that same fist, grabs a rattle and sticks it promptly into her mouth. Now she's decided that the rattle is also "me." Of course, still later, she'll have to come to terms with the fact that the rattle is a "not me," but the fist is still a "me." And she'll be doing that quite a bit for the next several years—determining through her own and others' responses, actions and reactions what is and is not "me."

We develop the ID, the mask and costume we will wear, by looking in the mirrors our primary caregivers, siblings and cultures provide for us. Of course, those mirrors are quite often made up of the dysfunction of those other humans in our lives and of our culture. But our psychology bounces off of this social interaction so that when we get consistent messages from others about who they need us to be, we believe that these messages must be true and act on them by fitting ourselves into a role that works for the interactions. Basically, the parents set the tone, so that if my parents see me as invisible then my siblings are likely to do the same. Then as I interact with my culture as an invisible person, they will begin to see me the same as well. So, let's play with that for a bit.

If as an infant my interactions with my parents or primary caregivers do not allow me to see myself as a visible entity with a personhood of my own, I might take on this invisible identity. I can see my hand, but not my face and my image of my body is relative to what I see in other's faces as I look to them for my mirror. But while my caregivers look at my lower body as they are changing my diapers, they rarely make eye contact with me and even more rarely talk to me. When I cry they are inconsistent with their responses so that I can't see the connection between my crying and their response to it. When I laugh they don't seem to notice much, and when I crawl, it all just seems very boring to them. When they hold me, my intuition, which is quite strong at this point, is picking up on their discomfort, their awkwardness, their wish to put me down. Soon, I'll be walking, but I do that because it is within me to do, not because of any notice I'll get from them. And I do that because to walk is to not have to be held, which relieves them of their discomfort.

As I move into toddlerhood, I am going to carry this invisibility with me, as it seems to be required by my parents and by now has become something of an identity that I can trust. I will, as most toddlers do, begin to experiment with my objective reality. Because I'm not getting noticed, these experiments may mean that I get hurt more frequently as I stumble through the world trying to find my way without guidance. The pain will be my teacher and I will most likely internalize this pain, making it the natural order of things, as it seems to be the only way I can learn about my environment. But this challenge will probably make me quite independent as I learn through the hard-knocks school. My verbal skills may suffer since I am not talked to very much, unless I have older siblings, but my independence may allow me to overcome that as well.

As I reach the age at which I will begin to play with peers, I am challenged with regard to my invisibility. Each time a peer attempts to interact with me, I am being given a choice as to how I will respond. Will I shoo them away with some overt gesture of anger? Will I just shyly retire from the interaction? Or, will I begin to experiment with these dynamics? Since I don't trust people to respond to me very well, I'm likely to choose one of the first two options.

That option continues to harden as I move into the school age years, in which I'll be confronted with the need to be socially savvy enough to make friends. Further, I'll be challenged as to how to succeed in school while remaining invisible. This means that I will most probably reject interaction with others as much as possible. But though I may feel very alone, as long as the tasks of learning can be done independently, I am likely to excel in these. In this case, I may be seen as a well-adjusted child who causes no trouble at school and works independently to make good grades. We do tend to evaluate our children according to their levels of achievement at school—a very poor assessment tool. What is actually happening in this case is that I'm being reinforced in my invisible role. If, however, I cannot do these tasks independently and alone, I may have to become an underachiever to stay under the radar. In this case, I'll probably have teachers hounding me to do better—which may make me develop a sense of guilt or shame.

As an invisible child I'll need to take one of three tacks. Either I am going to be quite busy with a lot of internal activity, like imaginary friends or lots of inner storytelling, etc. Or, I will cut myself off from internal activity, believing that to be visible to myself is frightening. Or, perhaps I will wiggle myself right into the medium between the two. Either way, no one else is invited into the inner sanctum to share the riches there. Regardless of whether or not I am excelling at school, on some level, either known or unknown to me, I feel utterly alone, and I do not let anyone know how difficult life is for me.

And then, I arrive at adolescence. Now I am going to be even further challenged, but I have become so well acquainted with my role, that I pretty much know what to do. I'll just do more of what I've always done. So, maybe I've done well in school, but I'm quite reserved and shut down when it comes to expression, and I trust no one. Now that the social challenge has ramped up its pressure, I'll trust people even less, shut down even more and try to achieve whatever I can by my own independent means. If I get a little taste of what it's like to relate to someone to whom I'm attracted, I might indulge, but I won't trust and I won't open up. And if I happen to run into some form of escape in which I can fall further into myself and away from others, I might indulge in that quite frequently.

Now some would say that what I've developed here is a personality. But if we are going to call this personality we have to keep in mind that there are many unexplored and definitely unexpressed parts of this personality. So, if personality is a mask and costume then yes, this is personality. But if personality is the healthy ego function of an authentic Self, then we are going to have to go a bit deeper. Still my role is clear. I'm invisible.

We can see that this identification or role started many years before when I was just an infant, and I found ways over the years to stay in it. That's how these identifications work. We tend to believe that we belong there and nowhere else. So, we will do just about anything, even distort reality, to stay in the role. In fact, these roles are our only sense of security. We tend to think that our security rests in how others treat us or in something like money. But that isn't really true. Our security rests in our identity. The identity allows us to always know how to respond to any given scenario—we just do what we've always done. It seems to us that there is no greater security than the sense that we always know what to do.

Even if what we've always done is worry, at least we know what to do. Even if the identity is the Victim role, it works in a strange uncomfortably comfortable way, simply because we know that we'll always be a victim and we just don't need to bother hoping for anything different. Besides, the Victim performance is very useful for getting others to take care of the poor Victim.

Now, of course, we are speaking of these identities in fairly one-dimensional language, though sometimes there is a combination of roles that we play. So, I can be the Superwoman and the Scapegoat. So now, I am not only motivated to do it all faster, higher, stronger than everyone else, complaining that they won't do it right because they are too slow, dumb or weak, but I also am motivated to do it all by guilt. That said, these identities or roles *can be* quite one dimensional. Again, you can learn much more about them in *Restoring My Soul: A Workbook for Finding and Living the Authentic Self*.

But underneath these roles is something more authentic. Something we knew about when we first came here, but something we put away in the closets of our minds, in order to be a part of life here on planet earth. We looked in the psychosocial mirrors around us and we adapted. The energy we have sent away into the unconscious is the I AM, the true Self, the soul. It is that essence of us that has never been wounded, and cannot, in fact, be wounded. It is our wholeness, our vitality, our freedom, our peace, our joy, our love and our wisdom.

The I AM is that within us to which Jesus referred as the kingdom of heaven within. And, as we shall see, in the next chapter, we are led to this essential nature by several of the other great traditions as well. It is very difficult, however, for us to believe in the I AM , mostly because what we see is what we've been taught to see—a misperception of who we are, and therefore, a misperception of our world. In fact, in many cases, we have adapted completely to the identity we adopted and the thought of losing it feels like fear of death.

Most of us were raised with an overdose of survival information. Not only were we shown how to survive in the world, but we sensed this fear of death all around us. In addition, in the primal archetypal regions of our instincts we knew as infants and toddlers that we needed our parents or caregivers desperately and that without them we would surely die. So, when they communicated to us what we should be, we found roles to fit into that agenda, in order to avoid their abandonment, thereby, keeping ourselves alive. And those who were abandoned before this bargain could take place often hardened into a cold shell, in which it seemed that the only bargaining chip left was an identification with rage, power and control.

Once we have successfully worn the role for a while, however, we've come to believe in it more than we believe in anything else. It is our security, our connection to family, and our hope of survival. Pretty powerful stuff. So, if we are somehow challenged, as we've seen that we quite often are, to take off the mask and costume, we will very often resist that shift in consciousness with tooth and nail. We might feel extremely frightened. We might feel as if we would be betraying our family system. We might even feel as if our lives are hanging in the balance.

But at every single juncture of our lives, in fact, sometimes daily, we are being so challenged. In the example above in which I played out the invisible role, every time someone in my class spoke to me I was challenged to take off the role and put on something more authentic. But how could I have known this? If I'd been tuned in to my inner dialogue, I would have noticed that there was one part of me that went directly to the invisible role without stopping to think about it; but there was another that was longing to speak to that person who just spoke to me. Over time this conflict could become apparent to me. But if I want to stay in the invisible role, then I'll have to blame the conflict on myself or others. I'll say, because I distrust them, that they are worthy of that distrust. It is their fault that I cannot speak to them. Or, I might say that there is something really wrong with me and that's why I can't talk when I want to, which of course makes it harder and harder to do so. Over time, these notions may build a thicker and thicker wall around me, so that I can maintain the role.

And, as we've said, it will take a crisis that is bigger than my fear of losing that role in order for things to begin to shift. So, if a crisis comes along that gets my attention, I may be pushed hard enough to want to peek beyond the role momentarily. But if the crisis subsides, I can just go back to same old same old. Or, if a crisis comes that I can blame yet again on others, then nothing has to change at all. Therefore, it may take a series of crises or it may take one enormous crisis that pushes me harder than my fear of changing frightens me.

If I can get it that I'm wearing the invisible mask and costume and that this mask and costume is keeping me from having a peaceful and fulfilling life, then I might begin to take the risks necessary to go a little deeper, to hear the voice of my soul calling me to those inner longings. But as I am taking those risks I am very vulnerable to any temptation that allows me to slide back into the role. So, if during the early stages of my risk taking, someone comes along who tells me I can have what I want if only I will start affirming and creating vision boards, then I might just fall back into my invisible role. Why? Because I can do these affirmations without ever having to take the risk to feel my feelings, understand my longings, or come to know how my role works and what triggers me to fall back into it. I can push my mind to think "positive" thoughts and struggle to avoid "negative" thoughts or feelings and simply repress my truest Self, yet again.

These roles run deep, and we are terrified of losing them. But it is these roles, these identities, which keep us stuck. We are not stuck because we lack faith, or because we haven't talked our thoughts into compliance with a regimen of "positive" thinking. We are stuck because we are stuck in an identity. And that identity is very often what has attracted the current crisis in the first place, through a long series of unconscious choices that have been based in identity. The current understanding of the law of attraction informs us that it is thought that created this crisis, as well as every other "negative" outcome in life. First, as we've said, chasing the so-called "negative" out of our lives with a "positive" chant, only serves to help us repress the "negative." And that "negative" will be one more barrier we will have to face as we walk into the shadows of the unconscious to find out who we are. Second, it is not thought that attracts, but identity, for it is in this root issue that we will find every single choice, both conscious and unconscious, that we have made, unless every now and then we got a wild hair and did something more authentic.

Yet going after the identity will not mean going up against it and trying to get it to go away. Anytime we go to war with something inside of us, be it an identity or a thought, in order to win that war, we have to repress the loser of the war. And again, when we want to find out who we are, as we walk through the doors to the unconscious, we are going to have to face that loser again in another war. In the same way that people don't get past addiction by simply saying "no" to it, we don't get past identity by simply saying "no" to it. We have to say "yes" to something else. And the "yes" is a hearty "yes" to our own authenticity. As I sit beside the mask and costume and simply listen to all of its urgent, desperate messages; and simultaneously sit with my Self and listen to all of its passion, its peace, it vital Life messages; I am much more likely to want more and more of the Self. Our current understanding of the law of attraction forbids this kind of listening.

It forbids it because it fears that if we listen to the "negative" we will give in to it. But mindfulness—or being the inner observer—does not mean we give in to anything. It only means that we are mindful. We absolutely can sit right in the middle of the divide inside of ourselves and do nothing but listen and observe. Whether we like to meditate or not, we can begin to listen. We can begin to sit within ourselves for periods of time during the day and just hear the messages clamoring for our attention. A message could be a body sensation, an uncomfortable feeling with which we might eventually become familiar enough to give it a name, like tension or that tightness we get when we are asked to do something we hate doing. A message could be an emotion, a dark mood, a feeling of lightness, a sense of calm and inner peace or even a dream. And we can have more than one message going on at the same time. But they are all messages. They want us to listen to what they have to say.

If we listen long enough we begin to associate certain feelings, sensations or even thoughts with certain messages. For example, fear messages might give us an entire laundry list of thoughts that explain why we should be afraid, but the feeling of fear is the same every time. Angry messages might tell us all the reasons why we should seek vengeance, but if we get into the observer mode, we might hear our anger telling us that there is a way in which we are neglecting our *own* needs and we must begin to pay attention.

For example, if I am angry at you because you are standing on my toe, but I haven't bothered to ask you to get off, then the problem isn't what you are doing so much as it is what I'm doing. But if I'm in the invisible role, then asking you to get off of my toe is going to make me visible, however briefly. I might feel intense fear about taking that risk. Yet if I'm in the observer mode, I'm just listening to the differing voices within me. When I get finished listening, because I've heard *all* of the voices—including the peaceful ones—I might be more willing to take that risk.

But if I'm told that I'm not supposed to pay attention to "negative" feelings, then I'm likely to not even know what is going on inside of me. How then will I know that you are on my toe? How will I find guidance as to what to do about it? And with regard to the law of attraction, how then will I know what to attract? More importantly, won't I just continue to attract the same old thing?

In the case of Alyson, whose fictional story we told in the previous chapter, we saw how listening to herself was the only way she was able to gain the clarity to put the past in the past where it belonged, and begin to develop the present her authentic Self desired. What we didn't see there is how she had attracted the husband and the life she had previous to her discovery of her Self. How did she end up with a husband who was so very much like her parents?

Roles are attracted to roles because they prop each other up. If I am living in the Victim identity, I am likely to attract either a Rescuer or a Bully, because these opposite roles allow me to feel safe in the only thing I understand, even if it isn't really safe. If I am living in the Good Guy Bargain and wearing the Scapegoat role, I am likely to attract someone who is a Blamer, so that I can continue to run myself by guilt, because it is guilt with which I am most familiar. If I am a Superwoman, I'm likely to attract a Big Baby type, who just won't grow up. That way I'll have someone to take care of, just like I took care of dear old Mom and Dad; and because Big Baby needs me he will not ever leave me. If I am a Runaway, I'm likely to become a serial monogamist at best.

Further, if I am a Rescuer, who else would I be interested in but someone who needs rescue? If I'm a Bully, I'll need to be with a partner I can bully. If I'm a Blamer, I'm going to need someone to blame—I mean you don't really expect me to admit I'm wrong do you? If I'm a Big Baby type, I've got to have a parental figure—usually a Superwoman or man. Otherwise, I'd have to grow up. Or, I might also be attracted to a Runaway, since neither of us really commit.

Now, many of us would say, "But I didn't know that she was in that role when we first met, and I was really attracted to her immediately." We tend to think about attraction as a conscious endeavor. But really, when was the last time you got up in the morning and said, "Today, I think I'll fall in love with someone," and you went and did it. That would be a conscious endeavor. Rather, falling in love seems to happen *to* us, seemingly out of the blue. Well, not really blue, just unconscious. We fall in love when something outside of us triggers an unconscious response inside of us—usually because the unconscious has been prepping us for that trigger before it occurred. This means that the more authentic we are the more likely we are to attract and be attracted to authentic externals.

But it also means that if what is outside matches an unresolved issue in the unconscious, we may be powerfully drawn to it. In Alyson's case, her unresolved issue was the fact that her parents did not take care of her or nurture her because of their addictions. Instead of resolving that issue, she'd masked it by playing a role. Her perspective husband "smelled" just like that issue when she first met him. I use the analogy of smell because the unconscious works in just that powerfully subtle way.

There was a certain delicious smell that pervaded my Nana's kitchen. When I smell that smell today, I am immediately thrown back into vivid memories of that place so that my body and mind feel as if they are actually there. Some smells take us directly to extremely difficult, even traumatic experiences. Sometimes we don't even recognize the triggering smell, but just find ourselves in this new emotional place. This is the way the unconscious works. It metaphorically "smells" a matching external and draws us to it. When Alyson met her prospective husband, she did not consciously know he had an addiction and lacked the capacity to really love and care for her, just like she did not consciously know all the myriad ways that playing Superwoman was helping her to cope with this lack in her parents. But her unconscious knew all of that. And it picked out the perfect candidate to help her to both marry her unresolved issues and present herself with an opportunity to resolve them.

The point of the unconscious urge is to present us with this opportunity. But on the conscious level, we think that the point is to get married. And so, we get involved with people who will help us to prop up our roles and live out the same dynamic we've always lived out. Somewhere along the way, hopefully, we will begin to realize what we are up to. In the meantime, we remain secure in the old identity. Remember that we said that there is no greater security than feeling that we always know what to do. Alyson knew what to do as Superwoman. In order for her to feel secure, she was going to have to be with someone who pushed her to be Superwoman, so that she could always know what to do. If she married someone who did not push her to be Superwoman she would not know what to do with that. So, she sought out a person who matched that unresolved material. This seeking is the same as attraction.

It is exactly the same with every other potential experience in life. We seek the money, the jobs, the circumstances, the health, the partners that match the identity. If the identity is the mask and costume then we will be attracted to the money, jobs, circumstances, health and partners that prop up the role. If the identity is the I AM, the authentic Self, then both the unconscious and the conscious are working on the same things. So, we will attract and be attracted to those things that match the I AM.

My identity is *meant* to match my authenticity. In other words we actually do have the capacity to live fully identified with the soul's truest nature. As we begin to live that way, we are in such constant access with the intentional power of the soul that it is now granted permission to give to our lives and our worlds all that matches that I AM. This is the true law of attraction at work. It might seem that we are attracting from the outer world all the light, love, wisdom and abundance that is natural to the soul. But in fact, the soul is *giving* light, love, wisdom and abundance *to the life.*

How then do we change the identity to that of the I AM? The most basic process is going to be accepting the life we have, the life that we have thus far given ourselves, as we saw Alyson accept her life. That acceptance stops the bargaining we've been doing for centuries. The old identity, the mask and costume and its role, *is* a bargain: *IF* I can put on this mask and costume and live out this scripted role, *THEN* I will be able to stay attached to these parents or this secure state. And it continues just that way with every other attachment. Acceptance moves us beyond bargaining for it takes a very hard look at reality and recognizes it, without minimizing, blaming, skirting or skewing—and then it just says, "Okay, that's how it is." It is within that process of acceptance that we are being granted the opportunity to go deeper, to begin to recognize the soul, to hear it, to listen to it and to honor its desires. And as we do that we *ensoul* the life, bringing the soul into body/mind awareness and activity, thus blessing the life with its true Life nature.

However, even when we begin to allow ourselves to recognize that we've been playing a role, bargaining with life and holding ourselves back from full throttle, the first thing we tend to do is beat ourselves up for not seeing it sooner. Here is where we get into criticizing, regretting, pushing and cajoling ourselves to be better people—to "self improve." And here is another spot where we are vulnerable to the influence of the old view of the law of attraction in which all we need to do is change our thinking, be more "positive" and everything will get better. If we try to do that we very often end up in the same fix later, but now with a whole lot more denial, because we don't want to think "negative" thoughts.

Of course, becoming conscious does often involve confronting the distorted thoughts we have about life, some of which can be quite destructive, but we must come to know those thoughts before we can confront them with their inaccuracy. That, however, is not the same as "self-improvement." Rather, such confrontation, such truth-telling would more accurately be called Self-alignment, because in becoming conscious of what is not true Self, we are also becoming conscious of what is true Self. Getting to know the authentic Self, the soul, the I AM is a journey. It is a journey that we will be taking for the entirety of our lives. For now, we only need to know that the *willingness* to look inside and see and hear what is in there is a huge part of it. And as we so open, we attract more and more openness. But if we stop short of that to engage in thought control, then we may be telling ourselves what to do, rather than listening to ourselves.

Telling ourselves what to do is an archetype of Western culture. It is a part of our apparent fear of the unknown—the deep and watery caverns of the internal. It amounts to a fear of the collective feminine. Western culture is built on the masculine archetype of structure, often rigid structure. We don't want life to be messy. We want order. We don't want to explore. We want to find. We don't want to crawl around in the leaky basements of our psyches. We want to be sure. We want to know what we are doing—which often amounts to staying with the familiar. In fact, we would often rather deal with a chaotic crisis then pay attention to its intuitive forewarning. Why? Because its intuitive forewarning is usually telling us to explore unknown regions of the inner being in order to learn something.

The feminine archetype, on the other hand, is receptive. It wants to receive before it gives. It wants to understand before it stands. It wants to wander around in the deep inner recesses of our being, touching and holding the various parts of the psyche until each part feels like a welcomed birth. It wants to allow each conception its time of gestation, and each new birth its time to suckle. It wants to continue to stay open and receptive to more information, more creativity, more.

After all of that, then the healthy masculine approach works. For it takes what has been received from within and walks out into the world with it. It takes the understanding and makes a stand. It knows when it is time to take up the pallet and walk. And it walks into the external and creates a similar world to that which has been found within.

The recent merging of Eastern and Western thought really can help us to incorporate both the feminine and the masculine approaches to our own humanity. But I'm afraid that our current understanding of the law of attraction was kidnapped at birth by the unhealthy masculine Western culture. And so we are forbidding ourselves to receive from within before trying to go out into the world. In fact, with our current understanding of the law of attraction, we are trying to attract from the external, by "correcting" the internal.

Our current way of understanding the law of attraction does not allow for life's circumstances to be fertile gestating fields of discovery given to us as a gift from the power of Life energy itself. Instead, it reduces all of our circumstances, relationships and life events, to a formula: "positive" thinking = "positive" results; "negative" thinking = "negative" results. In fact, it reduces it to a bargain—an attempt to control life. But what if Life was not meant to be controlled? What if the Life force both within and without has a whole other agenda than being controlled? What if mystery is a big part of that? What if we miss out on the sacred to the exact degree that we are trying to control our lives?

Life is a force that rolls around in us and runs through us. It is a force far bigger than that which our puny strategies for control can offer. It intends to carry us to the depths of its own mystery and it will not be stopped. So, when a crisis comes along and our aching hearts and hurt pride want to make the roller coaster stop, that might *not* be the next best thing for us. As I look back over my life at the various crises that got my attention, I realize now that it was like a bad dream that woke me up panting and sweating for that very purpose—to get my attention. And that attention had me looking and listening to myself in ways that I previously had not. Because I did look and listen, I am a whole other person today than I was before the crisis.

Isn't it possible that Life, the energy that is Life itself, runs the psyche toward wholeness? Isn't it possible that all of the unresolved material, suspended in the unconscious, utilizes all of that suspended Life energy to build to a crisis, in order to create the potential for resolution? And isn't it possible that each crisis pushes us closer to awareness of the river of Life flowing through it all? Isn't it possible that the long-term struggle we've had with money, for example, could be calling us to stop looking to money for life, but to look to Life for everything? Isn't it possible that under every life circumstance there is a Life energy that is ever creating newer and stronger awareness of the Soul nature?

The identity is *not* stronger than the authentic Self. The authentic Self is still putting us in the flow of its energy even when we don't know we are there. Even when the identity needs to channel the flow a certain way, still the flow and the river of Life cannot be stopped or even detoured for long. That river always comes from itself and goes to itself.

Have you ever noticed what happens to a stream of water when you put a large rock in it? The flow just moves around it. That's what happens to the river of Life when the identity or role becomes that rock. And it is just possible that the rock will be moved to another position entirely when the flow becomes strong enough to move it. Do we really imagine that our efforts to control our thoughts are going to push this enormous powerful river?

But we can learn to get into the flow of the river. We can learn to surrender our masks and costumes to the flow and just get in and ride. We can learn to stop being so afraid of surrender that we forget to Live. This will not happen because we try to control our thoughts. It will happen in a process of listening and observing what is inside of us. As we do, we get more and more comfortable with the topography around that river. And as we do that we get closer and closer to the edge of the river. By the time that we finally see it, all we want is to jump in. Jumping in that river is not throwing up a white flag that says "I surrender to my awful fate." It is just the recognition that the ego-states or roles do not have the final say. The truth is that *the soul, or authentic Self, is really always in charge; we just don't know it.*

The authentic Self, like another analogy, the roots of the tree, provides everything we need to Live, to thrive, to grow towards the sun. Have you ever seen a tree in the forest that starts growing from its root base, but then takes a hard right angle to the left or right, and then after a few feet of growth takes another hard right angle turn upward? When it took that first right angle turn, it was reaching over to where the sunlight fell. Once it found that place, it grew upwards toward the sun again. Quite intelligent, this tree!

We have the capacity to do that too. If the sun, or our sense of life energy, is blocked out by a bigger tree—very often primary caregivers—then the soul, our roots, allow us to bend so that we can capture the sun's rays. That bending is what the ego does when it forms a hardened ego-state—the mask and costume. We can come from our roots, but take a hard right angle turn to a whole other identity, and then once we have found a settled place with that identity, we just grow from there.

But the roots didn't stop being in charge of the tree's growth when it turned right or left. Rather, from its roots, the tree knew what to do. The roots sent energy that told the rest of the tree to live. Live! And something like instinct knew that the sunlight would make it live, so it reached for the light, thus bending in that hard right angle turn. In just this way, our authenticity is still in charge even when we make these hard right angle turns that keep us from being aware that we still come from our roots. But if we are going to surrender to the *real* law of attraction, that will be all about waking up to who is really running the show.

This does not mean that we go to war with the big "bad" ego in order to send it away. And it doesn't mean that we start controlling our thoughts. In fact, the minute we start trying to control anything, we are back in the ego-state. Even if we are trying to think "positive" thoughts that seem opposite from the ego-state, we are still working from the ego-state's understanding of life. And the bottom-line is that we are still working.

Every push we make to try to force ourselves into a certain frame of mind, *so that* we can accomplish a desired goal, is striving. We can strive after those "positive" thoughts and strive to put away those "negative" thoughts. Even in meditation we can be striving to control visualizations. Even as we *try* to relax we are striving after relaxation. But as we've said, we've been advised by sacred scripture to cease striving in order to know that we are God—in order to know the I AM that we are.

I AM is the power of that Universal energy—the very definition of our truest essence. ID, identity, makes us see through the eyes of whatever identification we carry. If we identify with the I AM, we see and our energy comes from the river of Life that has always been in charge all along. I AM is such power, such action, and such intention that we don't need to strive to attain anything. It will do all of the work within us and it will, of its own accord, give to our lives and to our world what it desires. Surrendering to the I AM nature within us is both letting go of the old ID, and falling into our own personal power. In fact, as we shall see from the next chapter, the I AM nature within us is the only true power.

6

What Do the Ancient Sacred Texts Really Tell Us?

Our first public initiation to what has become known as the law of attraction started when Esther Hicks channeled a group of entities or spirit guides called Abraham and she and her husband, Jerry, began to publish books about it that took off like wild-fire. And one of the most popular studies of that law has been found in the movie and book called *The Secret* by Rhonda Byrne.

Many of those who read and interpreted these and other works on the law of attraction are now telling us that the great spiritual traditions teach our current understanding of this law. But we are going to consider that idea now through what is written in several of the sacred texts of various world religions. Perhaps then, we can learn of the *true* nature of this law and how it works. For example, some of these folks quote the Buddha as having said:

> We are what we think. All that we are arises with our thoughts. With our thoughts we make the world (Chang 2006, 31).

Taken out of context, this statement would seem to support the current understanding of the law of attraction. But if what he meant was that we should use our thoughts to attract desirable external realities, then why did he say the following, taken from the *Surangama Sutra,* translated by Upasaka Lu K'uan Yu in 1966?

> You should know that the essential Bodhi is wondrous and bright, being neither cause nor condition, neither self as such nor not self as such, neither unreality nor not unreality, for it

> is beyond all forms and is identical with all things. How can you now think of it and use frivolous terminology of the world to express it? This is like trying to catch or touch the voice with your hand; you will not only tire yourself, for how can you catch the void (86)?

If it is true that the ultimate Bodhi, or the awakened person, is neither cause nor condition, then how is it that we think that we can cause an attraction with our thoughts—for to think thusly is to try to grab hold of the void.

When we put the first Buddha quote above into the context of the rest of Buddhist thought, we must conclude that he meant something other than that we should be using thought to attract our outer circumstances and our wealth. In fact, those who have studied Buddhism know that:

> Buddhist teachings emphasize mindfulness and acceptance of what *is*, instead of a constant focus on outcome, so that we can be free of suffering right now, not at some future point when we have the life we want (Erickson).

Here are just two of the many quotes from the Buddha about attachment found in the Dhammapada:

> Avoid attachment to both what is pleasant and what is unpleasant.... Clinging to what is dear brings sorrow. Clinging to what is dear brings fear. To one who is entirely free from endearment there is no sorrow or fear (Chang 2006, 60).

And:

> I have sons, I have wealth"—the fool suffers thinking thus. Even one's self is not one's own; how then sons, how then wealth (360)?

The Buddha's thoughts ran much deeper than the simplistic equation we find in the current understanding of the law of attraction. He constantly asserts that we must look within for everything; that our journey is not one relative to having, but to awakening to the riches and power found within us. In fact, he says, "…there is no grace, no help to be had from outside" (214).

So when we consider the term *thought* from a Buddhist perspective, we have to run deeper and longer to the ultimate conclusion. We might even wonder if his definition of *thought* was the same as our modern definition, for here is what he had to say about thoughts:

> In a pellucid ocean, bubbles arise and dissolve again. Just so, thoughts are no different from ultimate reality, so don't find fault; remain at ease. Whatever arises, whatever occurs, don't grasp—release it on the spot. Appearances, sounds, and objects are all one's own mind; there's nothing except mind (585).

Thoughts are impermanent because, according to this statement, they are but perceptions. If we agree with Buddhist philosophy, we are meant to release these thoughts immediately as they arise because they hold no more weight than a bubble rising in a pellucid ocean. If they are this inconsequential, why would they be powerful enough to attract? And it is this perception to which the first comment above refers when it says "we are what we think." We make our identities and our worlds of perception— all too often living in a perceived rather than a real world.

Not only that, but if thoughts were to be useful for attraction, such attraction would be considered to be attachment. And attachment would be seen as opposite of enlightenment:

> Those whose minds are well fixed upon the elements of enlightenment, who, without hankering after anything, glory

> in renunciation, whose biases are extinguished, who are full of light, they indeed have attained the bliss of Nirvana in this very world (263).

In this very world then, we are not to "hanker" for anything, according to Buddhism. We are to keep our sights set on the elements of enlightenment. But is the Buddha encouraging us to just separate ourselves from the world, have no connection to it, and take a vow of poverty, as some of Christian faith would put it? There are many who have interpreted his philosophy in this way.

What is it that people who come to Buddhism are seeking? Buddhist tradition answers that question by reminding us that it is actually the seeker who is being sought. The answer to the dilemma of attachment and its inherent suffering then is found in the Self. And yet the Buddhist tenet of *no-self* has to be considered as well. There are many different ideas about what this notion of self and no-self actually mean, but the clearest that I have found is in the concept of Tathagatagarbha, written about in the *Mahayana Mahaparinirvana Sutra* in which Tathagatagarbha is described as the true Self, the pristine Buddha nature—or the awakened nature—that lives within every person. But this true essence is hidden from most because we generally do not live from that place. This Sutra describes the Self as the real and the no-self as the unreal. The no-self would be somewhat equivalent to the identity with all of its attachments, or the perceptual world, as opposed to the essential living of Life that is the Self. The seeker then is actually seeking the true Self, which the Buddha thought of as eternal and boundless. And we shall see more of this eternal Self in other sacred texts from other world religions below.

If we put all of these Buddhist ideas together, what we must conclude is that any attachment to having is an attachment to that which is no-self, or not of the eternal Self. Those who then quote

Buddha as an example of a spiritual leader who believed in the current understanding of the law of attraction, either know nothing about Buddhist philosophy, are lacking insight into the meaning of these philosophies, or outright trying to mislead. While those who ascribe to the current understanding of the law of attraction will tell us that they advise people to "let go of outcomes," yet there is this striving after "positive" thinking meant to attract our dreams, which is also part and parcel of that understanding. And trying to find a place between the two poles of this double-speak amounts to a mechanical distraction when compared to the depth of insight necessary to true enlightenment.

The Bhagavad Gita is sacred Hindu scripture that tells the story of a conversation between the Hindu God Sri Krishna and the Prince Arjuna. It very clearly states in 12:12:

> Better indeed is knowledge than mechanical practice. Better than knowledge is meditation. But better still is surrender of attachment to results, because there follows immediate peace" (Easwaran 1985, 2007, 208).*

Has some of our affirming and vision boarding turned into mechanical practice? A bigger question: How does one surrender attachment while striving not to think "negative" thoughts and think only "positive" thoughts *in order* to have something? Isn't it possible that while we striving, we are missing out on the knowing that can only occur when we live deep in the inner life of the Self? In 4:9-10 of the Bhagavad Gita, we read:

> Those who know me as their own divine Self break through the belief that they are the body and are not reborn as separate creatures. Such a one, Arjuna, is united with me. Delivered from selfish attachment, fear, and anger, filled with me, surrendering themselves to me, purified in the fire of my being, many have reached the state of unity in me (117).*

This could not be clearer. We are here to be. To become *Being*—to know the self as Divine Self. This Beingness is the knowledge referred to in 12:12. And, according to the above, it is such Beingness that "delivers us" from attachment, fear and anger. So when we consider the current understanding of the law of attraction from this perspective, we may conclude that what we need to be "attracting" is an awareness of who we are as Divine Beings. And once we know that, there is yet more to be known, for 9:4-5 tells us this:

> I pervade the entire universe in my unmanifested form. All creatures find their existence in me, but I am not limited by them. Behold my divine mystery (173)!*

If we are at essence, indeed, the Divine Self, then we pervade the entire universe in our unmanifested form, and we are likewise pervaded by the Divine. All creatures find their existence in us, as we find ours in them. This is, indeed, a Divine mystery, to which the law of attraction, as we currently understand it, does not do justice. We are so much more than mere creatures who are striving to stay alive and find some way to be happy here on this planet. The current understanding of the law of attraction limits us to that striving, for it puts us in a narrow place in which only "positive" thinking, feeling and imaging can get us what we want. But we can see here that this sacred text supports a way of Being that runs much deeper than that. And yet there is more, for in 11:38, we read:

> You are the knower and the thing which is known. You are the final home; with your infinite form you pervade the cosmos (200).*

Arjuna is speaking here to Krishna, or Divine Self, and declaring that all true knowledge comes from Divine Self and all that can be known is Divine. That is true because Divine Self is our own infinite home. This is the same idea, as we shall later see, put forth by Jesus when he declares that the kingdom of heaven is within us. And the Bhagavad Gita describes the nature of that Divine Self (2:23-30):

> The Self cannot be pierced by weapons or burned by fire; water cannot wet it, nor can the wind dry it.... It is everlasting and infinite, standing on the motionless foundations of eternity.... The glory of the Self is beheld by a few, and a few describe it; a few listen, but many without understanding. The Self of all beings living within the body, is eternal and cannot be harmed. Therefore do not grieve (91-92).*

So, now here is the question: If it is true that we are Divine Self, that we are pervaded by the Divine and likewise pervade all things as Divine Beingness, that we are everlasting, infinite and cannot be harmed, then why do we need to attract anything from the external to attain fulfillment? Here is the answer to that question, found in 4:11-12 of the Bhagavad Gita:

> As they approach me, so I receive them. All paths, Arjuna, lead to me. Those desiring success in their actions worship the gods; through action in the world of mortals, their desires are quickly fulfilled (117).*

The answer is that no matter what we do we are always moving toward full awareness of the Divine Self. The answer is that we can easily attain success on planet earth through our actions, but there is so much more that is actually going on here, for we see in 4:12-18 that:

> The distinctions of caste, guna, and karma have come from me. I am their cause, but I myself am changeless and beyond

> all action. Actions do not cling to me because I am not attached to their results. Those who understand this and practice it live in freedom.... The wise see that there is action in the midst of inaction and inaction in the midst of action. Their consciousness is unified, and every act is done with complete awareness (117-118).*

The Divine Self within us is beyond all action, yet it acts with inaction. This is another way of talking about effortless effort. When we are operating from complete awareness in everything we do, it is because we have first accessed the Divine Self and become congruent with it so that it can then act in and through us, and we operate out of effortless effort.

The current and common understanding of the law of attraction tells us to change our thoughts to "positive" thoughts and our emotions to "positive" emotions without first telling us to find and begin to live out of the Divine Self. When we follow these tenets we get very busy with having in order to become, rather than simply becoming. When we operate from the Divine Self, everything about us runs much deeper than the tenets of our current understanding of the law of attraction can even reach. And though ultimately it will still lead to the same outcome—as we saw above in 4:11-12—if our effortless efforts were all about union with the Divine Self, they would describe a completely different life.

The secret that had to be told to Arjuna in the Bhagavad Gita is this simple fact: Our journey is about uniting individual consciousness with the Ultimate Consciousness of Divine Self. Whether we have or don't have, whether we strive or don't strive, whether we use the action that leads to quick success or we unite action with inaction, whether we use the current understanding of the law of attraction or we revise that understanding now and go straight for Ultimate Consciousness—all paths inevitably lead to that Ultimate Consciousness.

But if we wish to utilize the *true* law of attraction, then our journey will not be about trying to figure out how to attract the things we think we want and need from the external world. It will be about finding out who we really are! But when I say this, those who espouse the current understanding of the law of attraction very often become quite concerned that I am telling them that they should take some kind of vow of poverty and forego any effort in the direction of their dreams. This is black and white thinking: Either we have it all, or we should have nothing.

But that is not at all what is meant. Ultimate Consciousness does not ask that we live in a rarified plane, separated out from the things of this world. Ultimate Consciousness wishes to fully embody the things of this world! But in order for us to consciously allow that awareness in our own lives, we must surrender to union with the Ultimate Consciousness of Divine Self with our own bodies and minds. This union is not a half-hearted union, so that we say that we are One with the Divine, but don't live as such. Rather it is a *Life* in and of itself. All we do is join that Life and we are automatically in the flow, in the essence of all things. If true desire comes to us then, it is a part of the creative design of Divine Beingness, and will bring about its intention through the fact that it pervades all things.

As long as we are putting our energy behind attracting, we are assuming that the possession of that object of desire is going to make us happy. Leo Buscaglia said it best in his book *Love*:

> In actuality, no man possesses anything but himself.... One can hold on to nothing or no one. (Chang 2006, 362).

If the only thing we own is ourselves, and the self we own awakens to Divine Self, and that Beingness pervades all things, isn't this everything we need and desire?

The same idea is put forth by Jalaluddin Rumi, a poet and Sufi mystic of the thirteenth century. Sufism is the mystical dimension of Islam. Rumi had this to say about how we live here on planet earth:

> Live in the nowhere that you come from, even though you have an address here (223).

What could this strange statement mean? Well, the first thing we can clearly see is that it doesn't mean that we should spend our days striving to attain through the power of "positive" thinking. It seems to mean that we should be living, not from our address here, not from our identifications with the culture and its assigned roles, but from that Ultimate Consciousness referred to in the Bhagavad Gita. This is clarified by the following encouragement, also by Rumi:

> Every morning a new arrival…a joy, a depression, a meanness …welcome and entertain them all! (23).

Again, it is clear that this statement doesn't mean that we should awaken and meditate for five to ten minutes on our desires, and think only "positive" thoughts all day. Rather, when we are identified with the Divine Self, we can accept and receive with love and attentiveness *any* thought or feeling that arises. And we can do that with complete freedom from the fear that if we do, we will attract "negative" energy.

From the "Don't Listen to the Trickster" Odes in *Teachings of Rumi,* by Andrew Harvey, we have this insight:

> The whole of life is now, is today, is this eternal moment (572).

This means so much more than just "living in the moment," the buzz-phrase of pop culture in which we just go with our general impulses. It means that there is such a thing as an "eternal moment." The eternal moment is the blending of past, present and future. It is the blending of earth consciousness with Ultimate Consciousness, ego-state with Divine Self, in which we recognize the genuine beauty and amazing love that exists within us at the juncture of that blend. The phrase *eternal moment* would otherwise be an oxymoron. If, however, we listen to the trickster, we assume that we will only have an abundant life *if* we can think "positive" thoughts long and hard enough to attract our dreams.

And finally, from the *Pocket Rumi Reader* by Kabir Helminski, and the poem "Mature Yourself":

> No mirror ever became iron again;
> no bread ever became wheat;
> no ripened grape ever became sour fruit.
> Mature yourself and be secure
> from a change for the worse.
> Become light (715).

First, this statement has nothing to do with building our lives from the outside in. Rather, it intimates that what we are building is ourselves. We are in a process of realization that comes from the inside and brings us to the light. But what is it that Peter Pan says to Wendy, John and Michael to get them to fly away to Never-Never Land with him?

> You must think lovely, wonderful thoughts and they will lift you up in the air ~ J.M. Barrie, *Peter Pan* (702).

Peter Pan, the expert in "I won't grow up," I won't develop maturity, tells us to think lovely thoughts, think only "positive" thoughts, so that we can fly away to Never-Never-Land.

I'm sorry to say that so many of us have spent years attempting to think only "positive" thoughts and refusing to allow "negative" thoughts or feelings, but haven't yet attracted those results we were looking for. And while we know that we aren't supposed to be attached to outcomes, and we strive to also let go of those, the entire energy is based on the bargain that IF we can have what we fancy, THEN we will finally be happy. And this psychology removes us from the eternal moment, and keeps us stuck in the fantasy of having rather than Being. In fact, it is a very short trip to Never-Never-Land.

But, again, this doesn't mean that we don't also have as a part of Being. We can see this clearly in the Old Testament of the Christian Bible and the Ketuvim of the Tanakh of the Hebrew Bible.

> Cast your bread on the surface of the waters, for you will find it after many days (Ecclesiastes 11:1).

What does this strange instruction mean? Taken literally it could mean something about throwing away our food in faith that it will return to us. But in order to understand this verse we have to read verses 4 and 5 of the same chapter:

> He who watches the wind will not sow and he who looks at the clouds will not reap. Just as you do not know the path of the wind and how bones are formed in the womb of the pregnant woman, so you do not know the activity of God who makes all things.

Ultimately the writer of Ecclesiastes is telling us of the futility of living as if we can control life. For this dilemma the author recommends that we simply recognize the mystery of living and surrender to it. So, when we cast our bread upon the surface of the waters, the mystery is that it returns to us. Both bread and water are metaphorical equivalents of spiritual and physical sustenance. Such casting then implies surrender to that mystery. And the mystery that has already been explained to us is that all is One. Therefore, there is no separation between me and my bread—so why would it not return to me when I cast it into the flow?

Surrender is something about which the current and common understanding of the law of attraction has completely forgotten. And we must admit that the term has certain fundamentalist connotations. But this kind of surrender is not related to religion. It is related to the Ultimate Consciousness of Beingness. When we fully surrender to Beingness we entrust everything to the Ultimate Consciousness that we are Divine Beings. We surrender to our own essence.

The enlightened understanding of the above verses goes hand-in-hand with the one found in Proverbs 3:9-10:

> Honor the LORD from your wealth, and from the first of all your produce; so your barns will be filled with plenty and your vats will overflow with new wine.

Most often this verse is interpreted to mean something about tithing, so that IF we give the tithe of first fruits to God, THEN God will give us abundance. Those who push for tithing, even in the most liberal of churches, do not realize the bargaining in this kind of thinking. Verses like this one are interpreted to mean that there is an IF/THEN relationship between the Divine and humanity. That thinking is part of the problem that we find in the current understanding of the law of attraction. Can it really be true that God, the Divine, the Universe, Spirit, or whatever name we give this Ultimate Consciousness, would only provide for us in the event that we, in our puny little ego-states, would give something in exchange for that provision? How very small-minded and ego-centered this Ultimate Consciousness would be if that were so.

Rather this verse has, again, to do with surrender. *The first of our produce is the realization that we are Divine Beings.* We honor the Lord with our wealth when we realize that there is nothing that isn't already ours. Thus our barns are filled to overflowing. And again we see this same theme in Proverbs 11:24-25:

> There is one who scatters, yet increases all the more, and there is one who withholds what is justly due, but it results only in want. The generous man will be prosperous and he who waters will himself be watered.

From a literal interpretation, this verse seems to be telling us what those who espouse the current understanding of the law of attraction tell us: Give generously and you will receive generously. While giving generously is definitely something we can continue to enjoy doing, if we are doing it in order to receive generously, then we are bargaining yet again. But surrender to Ultimate Consciousness means that we realize that there is absolute freedom in giving ourselves completely to the Universe, for we are One with all. And we are made prosperous because there is no lack in Oneness. There cannot be.

This is in complete agreement with Jesus' later sermon in which he said:

> For this reason I say to you, do not be anxious for your life, as to what you shall eat; nor for your body, as to what you shall put on. For life is more than food, and the body than clothing. Consider the ravens, for they neither sow nor reap; and they have no storeroom nor barn; and yet God feeds them; how much more valuable you are than the birds! And which of you by being anxious can add a single cubit to his life's span? If then you cannot do even a very little thing, why are you anxious about other matters? Consider the lilies, how they grow; they neither toil nor spin; but I tell you, even Solomon in all his glory did not clothe himself like one of these. But if God so arrays the grass in the field, which is alive today and tomorrow is thrown into the furnace, how much more will He clothe you, O men of little faith! And do not seek what you shall eat, and what you shall drink, and do not keep worrying. For all these things the nations of the world eagerly seek; but

> your Father knows that you need these things. But seek for His kingdom and these things shall be added to you. Do not be afraid little flock, for your Father has chosen gladly to give you the kingdom (Luke 12: 22-32).

Life is more than food and the body more than clothing. Life is that river that flows beneath everything we do, say and think. Life is that essential fire within us that never goes out. If this is true, how could it be that Life can be scarce, can suffer lack, can go about naked? Notice here that Jesus does not say IF we think "positive" thoughts THEN we will wear clothes finer than those worn by Solomon. He does not say IF we do a vision board and work to visualize our dreams twice a day THEN we will be fed and clothed mentally, emotionally, physically and spiritually. He simply says that this is our right, for we are One with Ultimate Consciousness, the Divine Self, what he would call the "Father." We are One with that Life that is more than food.

But that is far from all that is said here, for here, in these verses we learn where the focus of the law of attraction should be. We are to seek the kingdom of heaven—referred to in other Gospel texts as the kingdom of God. And yet even that seeking is not to be made up of striving—for "the Father" has already given it to us. We already have the kingdom of God within us, but when we turn to look at it, our provision becomes visible.

We can know this is so because Jesus very clearly answered those who accused him of blasphemy thusly:

> "Has it not been written in your Law, 'I said you are Gods?'"(John 10:34).

He was referring to the scripture of Psalm 82:6:

> I said you are Gods, and all of you are sons of the Most High.

It is interesting that traditionalists tend to take so much of sacred scripture literally, but verses that so clearly tell us who we are and where the focus of our attention needs to be are simply ignored, or if they are noticed, are not taken seriously at all. When Jesus responded to his accusers this way, he was basically saying even his accusers were Divine. Why would he have given them such power if he just wanted to mentally twist their laws in order to defend his own behavior—one common interpretation of his remarks?

In fact, he is saying the exact same thing as we read earlier in Buddhist, Sufi, and Hindu texts: We are One with the Divine. And it is knowledge of this Oneness—not mere intellectual knowledge, but deep, abiding inner knowing—that allows us to have all that is owned, loved and nurtured by the Divine. This is what is meant by the parable of the mustard seed in which Jesus said (Mark 4:30-32):

> ...How shall we picture the kingdom of God, or by what parable shall we present it? It is like a mustard seed, which, when sown upon the soil, though it is smaller than all the seeds that are upon the soil, yet when it is sown, grows up and becomes larger than all the garden plants and forms large branches; so that the birds of the air can nest under its shade.

Our tiny glimmers of recognition of who we are will ultimately become complete consciousness of Divine Self, and when they do, every single transcendent thought, feeling and action we've ever had will come to roost in the branches of that Ultimate Consciousness. And this is exactly what he meant when he referred to the kingdom of heaven or the kingdom of God as residing within us (Luke 17:20-21):

> Now having been questioned by the Pharisees as to when the kingdom of God was coming, he answered them and said,

> "The kingdom of God is not coming with signs to be observed, nor will they say, 'Look, here it is!' or 'There it is!' For behold, the kingdom of God is *within you*." (Emphasis on the literal translation).

Just as the Bhagavad Gita declared that Ultimate Consciousness pervades all things and that all roads lead to that Ultimate Consciousness of Divine Self, Jesus is here declaring that the kingdom of heaven or God is found within us. There is no external sign, event, circumstance or goal—whether or not it is on our vision boards—which will bring about a heaven on earth. This is an inside job. But, because Ultimate Consciousness pervades all things, *whatever we experience*, we are experiencing Divine Self. The only question is whether or not we know it.

Further, this is exactly what Jesus was talking about when he made the following statements:

> Truly, truly, I say to you, he who believes in Me, the works that I do shall he do also; and greater works than these shall he do, because I go to the Father (John 14:12).

> Truly, I say to you, if you have faith and do not doubt... even if you say to this mountain, 'Be taken up and cast into the sea,' it shall happen (Matthew 21:21).

These verses and others like them are traditionally interpreted to mean that we should have faith in Jesus or in God and that when we do our requests will be honored. But if we are the Gods he says we are, then when we "believe in Me" what we are believing in is the I AM, the fact of our own Divine nature, so exemplified in Jesus.

And finally Jesus had this to say in response to his disciples' question, "How will we know the way?":

> *I AM* the way, and the truth and the life; no one comes to the Father, but through Me (John 14:5-6, *emphasis added*).

He didn't mean that we were to worship him as the only son of God, thereby depriving ourselves of our own I AM—for if he did, why would he have also told us that we would do greater works than he? He meant that as we see the Divine in him, we are also seeing the Divine in us, and so it is that we have the way, the truth and the Life. He meant that the I AM within him was the same as the I AM within us, and that I AM is the way, the truth and the Life.

These verses have been so cluttered with Christian dogma, that we have missed the fact that they are clearly telling us about the law of attraction. Yet they are giving us an entirely new version of that law: "Seek His kingdom and these things will be added to you," for "You are Gods!" What we are learning here is that sacred scriptures from around the world are all telling us the same thing. "The kingdom of God," "I AM," "Divine Self," "Ultimate Consciousness" and "Tathagatagarbha" are all synonymous terms!

Our only job then is to find the sacred Self. Buried deep under the masks and costumes, under the internalized societal norms, and familial demands, under all the "wants" that are mere compulsions, under all the "needs" that are based on fear, under all the ego-state-driven demands to have rather than to be—under all of that, we find the Divine Self. *And then*, all those other things are added to us. They can be added to us, because they *are* us.

One of my favorite verses from the book of Psalms is this one:

> For every beast of the forest is Mine, the cattle on a thousand hills.... If I were hungry, I would not tell you; for the world is mine and all it contains (Psalms 50:10-12).

Here we are clearly being told that we do not have a bargaining relationship with the Divine. The Divine does not need us to feed some fragile Superpowered ego, so that we can have our needs met. The Divine needs no sacrifices. More than that, if we are One with the Divine, then the cattle on a thousand hills are also ours. But as we saw in the Gospel verses above, we must believe this, in order for it to be true *for us*. In order to awaken to the river of Life that is always flowing through us and in us, we must come to know, as Jesus knew. And what Jesus knew was this:

> I can do nothing on My own initiative. (John 5:30).

> Jesus therefore said, "When you lift up the Son of Man, then you will know that I am *He*, and I do nothing on My own initiative, but I speak these things as the Father taught Me" (John 8:28).

The italicized *He* in John 8:28 is a word that was not really there in the original text but implied by it, according to the explanation of the format in *The Hebrew-Greek Study Bible, New American Standard Version,* from which this text was taken. But the terms *I AM* are clear from such implications. This verse tells us that when we lift up humanity to its truest nature, we find the I AM. But more than that, that I AM is synonymous with the Father—the river of Life that flowed through Jesus—so that what appeared to be effort on his part was actually the Divine moving within and through him. Here Jesus is telling us that when we live in the I AM energy, we do not act on the ego-state's initiative, but rather all action comes from the flow of the Divine Self. And *this* is the law of attraction in action, for each Divine initiative accomplishes what it set out to do.

Since our current understanding of the law of attraction does not first instruct us to realize our Oneness with the Divine, it encourages us to operate out of ego initiative to think "positive" thoughts and renounce all "negative" thoughts and feelings—even as it simultaneously tells us to get rid of ego. But if Jesus did not operate out of his own initiative, though he was one of our models of Divine Self, then why is it that we think that we are to initiate this enormous effort to bargain with life. Rather we are meant to surrender, to fall into the flow of energy that springs eternal from the authentic and Divine Self, the soul, the Ultimate Consciousness.

Basically then what we have discovered is that the current understanding of the law of attraction does not take us far enough into the truth. The Buddha said:

> There are only two mistakes one can make along the road to truth; not going all the way, and not starting" (Chang 2006, 720).

We have made a good start with the current understanding of the law of attraction, but we have not gone all the way along the road to truth. The work necessary to the current understanding of the law of attraction is a bargain that has us struggling to put our heads in a narrow place in which there is room enough only for our definition of "positive," to draw from the external world our happiness. But if the seeker is that which is actually being sought, then what we long for in the external world is but a metaphor for the longing we have for the Self. Yet, the paradox is that the Self is in everything, so that once we are clearly identified with that Self, we also realize that our barns are full to overflowing.

* From *The Bhagavad Gita,* translated by Eknath Easwaran, founder of the Blue Mountain Center of Meditation, copyright 1985, 2007; reprinted by permission of Nilgiri Press, P. O. Box 256, Tomales, CA 94971, www.easwaran.org

7

Getting I AM Out of the Shadow

The concept of the shadow is relatively new to us. Until Freud's ideas about the unconscious came into public awareness, our thoughts about it were largely philosophical. But even Freud did not call the unconscious *the shadow*. That was Jung. By now it is common knowledge that Carl Jung originally followed Freud's theories on the unconscious, but eventually broke away from Freud and formulated his own theories. Freud's theory was that the unconscious was formed of repressed wishes, but Jung, who spent the rest of his life investigating the unconscious and its contents, came to believe that within every individual there is both a collective unconscious and a personal unconscious.

The collective unconscious is like a "universal library of human patterns of behavior, or the Sage in every man" (Carl Jung Resources). It works in collaboration with the personal unconscious, but the collective unconscious is somewhat different in that it offers us archetypes.

> Archetypes constitute the structure of the collective unconscious—they are psychic innate dispositions to experience and represent basic human behavior and situations. Thus mother-child relationship is governed by the mother archetype. Father-child—by the father archetype. Birth, death, power and failure are controlled by archetypes. The religious and mystique experiences are also governed by archetypes. The most important of all is the Self, which is the archetype of the center of the psychic person, his/her totality or wholeness (Carl Jung Resources).

The personal unconscious, on the other hand, is filled with forgotten, ignored or repressed experiences of all kind—including physical, emotional, mental and spiritual experiences. But since both the collective unconscious and the personal unconscious reside within an individual mind, it can be somewhat difficult to sort out the distinctions, especially given the fact that when archetypes of the collective unconscious are triggered they can create quite a powerful personal response. Further, several of the archetypes that are formed in the collective unconscious are very personal including those with which we might personally identify. These include mother, father, sister, brother; the anima (the feminine archetype), the animus (the masculine archetype), and the Self (the authentic Self), as well as the archetypes of victim, scapegoat, superhuman, etc.

Recently, and largely because of the Human Potential movement, some of Jung's theories have become mainstream. In fact, many of his archetypes have been so included in mainstream pop culture, that we find male sit-com comedians regularly poking fun at their "feminine side," and people randomly referring to the shadow as if it were an inner demon of sorts. Because this is true, many of these archetypes have been diluted, even drained of significant power in order to fit into mainstream thought. One of those archetypes, the shadow itself, has become quite significant to some alternative practitioners as they advise their clients, who are having trouble with activating the principles of the current understanding of the law of attraction. But the version of the shadow that is used is the diluted one, so that its definition is now dumbed down to consist of a darkness or "negativity" within the mind of humanity that causes us to misbehave.

This means that when the concept of "getting rid of ego" doesn't seem to work, many who teach the current understanding of the law of attraction are advising their clients to find the material in the shadow that is blocking them from attaining their dreams. It is thought that what is lurking in the hidden regions of the psyche is some old unresolved conflict from childhood, or some dark "negative" side of the self that is holding us back and holding us down. While it is true that many of us carry unresolved issues around with us, both consciously and unconsciously, the object of this well-intended advice is to "clear" the psyche of these issues or blocks.

But this notion, like the idea of "getting rid of ego," has as its base, a faulty premise. Just as the concept of getting rid of ego is ineffective and even dangerous, so clearing out the shadow is, likewise, ineffective and dangerous. First, if something is unconscious it is so for a reason. And second, this very mechanical and contrived method of working with the enigmatic power of the psyche is reductionist at best and at worst could be quite damaging.

I hear these stories frequently from readers, listeners and clients, who tell me that they are striving to "bring consciousness" to their efforts to attain their dreams. By this they mean that they are going to get rid of ego and clear the blocks hidden in their shadow material. And they must do this very quickly, in order to "accelerate" their growth so that they can attain their dreams. Actually, they spend a lot of time quarreling with the ego or the shadow, and undergo frequent bouts of shame, because they have not yet been able to get rid of ego and overcome the shadow blocks. And they want me to please explain to them what they are doing wrong. Many of these people were already troubled before they read about the law of attraction and they have become even more troubled as they try desperately to lay aside their original problems through "positive" thinking.

Because the current understanding of the law of attraction does not first advise that we seek the Self, the so-called "dreams" that these persons have invested in could be and very often are fantasies based on old identities. When we are not closely allied with the soul, we often do not yet grasp true soul longings. But someone told these people that the law of attraction was the way to make everything right in their lives, and they desperately needed to believe it—so they did. Therefore, their dreams are quite often of fantastic proportions making them the best, the highest, the noblest, the richest and the most powerful—oh, and by the way, the most loving—for they have learned from their teachers that to wish for less is a sign of fear of success. They do not see troubles and crises as midnight friends who come to guide them deeper into themselves. No, troubles and crises are just more evidence that they are doing it all wrong. Troubles and crises have come to tell them that they are still attracting "bad" stuff, that they are not doing the attraction work "right," because if they were, they would not be attracting these things.

They see the ego as "bad," because it is that thing that has learned to think "negative" thoughts and become a part of the world's "negative" energy. And the shadow is even worse, for in it lurks all of the stuff that the ego didn't want to deal with. Now enter the healer, whose intention it is to pull all of that "bad" stuff out of the shadow and render it powerless over the person's life. While I must hasten to say that there are many healers who offer genuine and compassionate healing services, there are also those horror stories that come back to me from clients, listeners, workshop attendees and readers. Some of these follow—specifically, those related to the current understanding of the law of attraction. Each case described represents several stories combined into one fictitious person.

Susan was told by her healer and life coach, Tony, that she was abused as a child, and that it was this abuse and Susan's attachment to it that was creating the manifestation problem. Susan came to therapy to work on the history of abuse. But as she told her life story, she would often say, "...and Tony told me that I..." as if Tony knew more about her life than she did. In the name of trying to make her dreams come true, Susan had given herself entirely to someone who defined her instead of helping her find herself.

Slowly as I began to ask Susan more and more about her own thoughts and feelings, not allowing her to tell me what Tony thought or felt, she gained enough ground so that I could ask her what she remembered about having been abused. "Oh," she said, "I don't remember it at all. Tony told me that I've been abused and that this abuse, hidden in my shadow, is what is keeping me from attracting my dreams." Gently, I asked if Susan knew what clues Tony had put together to give him this information. She doesn't know, but Tony is psychic and she trusts him. So, the work of therapy is cut out for us. We are going to have to start all over with Susan, helping her to first come to terms with more of her own thoughts and opinions and then to help her decide for herself if she thinks she's been abused or not. What we want is for Susan to put her own feet on the ground instead of trying to walk on Tony's. For only in so doing will Susan be able to find her own Self—which is the true goal of the law of attraction.

Another fictitious combination of stories is represented by Jon, who actually *was* abused as a child but told by his healer that until he could forgive and forget about the abuse, he would not attract his dreams. Jon was instructed to go to his perpetrator, his father, who was now in jail, and tell him that he forgave him, and that in so doing, he would be set free to manifest his own dreams. He did as he was instructed but, instead of coming out filled with peace as he'd been told he would, he came out feeling intense anger. When he reported this to his so-called healer, he was told that he must stop feeling angry, for only then would he be able to manifest his dreams. They did some "healing work" on his anger, in which Jon was not permitted to see or clarify what was going on in his own psyche, but which was meant to "release" or "cleanse" that "negative" anger.

In the end, however, Jon was left with having to stop up his anger in order to please his healer. Eventually he was able to repress those feelings, but found himself shortly thereafter, in yet another abusive relationship with a partner who reminded him very much of his original abuser. And of course, he was told that he'd attracted this relationship and that this fact was evidence that he was still carrying around some anger in his shadow. Jon had continuously repeated in his relationships the traumas of his childhood. But this was *not* because he was attracting it through the power of "negative" unforgiving energy, but because he had unresolved issues that were seeking resolve through falling in love with people who were just like dear old Dad.

The fact is that if Jon is falling in love with people like his father, this is evidence of the, perhaps unconscious, unconditionality of his love for his father. The problem wasn't that he didn't love and have compassion for Dad, but that he had defined *himself* in some way relative to the abuse he had received. One of the bargains we often make as children who are abused is: IF I can take on the guilt, THEN I can still believe that Dad is good and will take care of me. Children do this because realizing that Dad is really doing something very harmful to them makes them believe that they might not survive childhood. Remember that the primary strength given to a child is his imagination. He is using that imagination to save his own life, or at least to give himself the illusion that he is saving his own life, by pretending that he must be the problem and that IF only he could be good enough, THEN his perpetrator would be the good caregiver he needs him to be.

So, Jon had defined himself as unlovable and worthy of the abuse he was given, and until he went to see his Dad in jail, and felt the enormous anger at his father, he'd never really thought of his father as the problem. He'd fallen in love again and again with women who treated him the same way his father did, because he was still trying to maintain that magical relationship with his fantasy father through these other relationships. In fact, it was his anger that was the beginning of his healing, for in that anger he was about to find the internal power to protect himself from ever letting this happen again. But instead, he was told to put away that "negative" anger, doing the same old thing he'd been doing all of his life, yet one more time—and THEN maybe he could finally manifest his dreams. The issue here is obviously not one in which Jon needs to work on forgiving his father, but one in which he unburies himself from years and years of bargains, in which Dad was easy to forgive, but Jon was not.

Finding out who we are is not a job that we do *in order* to fulfill dreams that we fantasized *before* we ever found out who we were. Finding out who we are is a journey into ourselves that begins with brave curiosity and ends with consciousness of enormous Self-love. We don't take those journeys lightly. In fact, as we've already said, they are often very frightening to us. And we certainly don't need to be shoved onto the path by someone who tells us that unless we hurry up and get all this garbage cleaned out, we are never going to be happy, fulfilled people.

I've heard of cases in which gays or lesbians were told by healers that they were of the opposite gender in a previous life and that the reason that they *felt* gay or lesbian was because they were simply longing to go back to that other gender. They were told that they needed to do a past-life regression in order to let go of the previous gender identity so that they could get on with living true to the body they had been given in this life. This thinly-veiled homophobic response was basically informing these people that their authentic sexual orientation was the reason that they were not attracting the money and jobs that they wanted.

All of these mistakes were made in the name of rushing people into dealing with deep psychic issues in order that they might hurry up and have their dreams. Not only were they being rushed, but they were being rushed to do all the wrong things. These attempts are not only wrong-headed, but they miss the entire point of the true law of attraction which is, as we said in the previous chapter, the seeker.

Journeys into the psyche should be made with gentleness, quietness, self-compassion and a great deal of respect for mystery. Jerking the psyche into position to attract one's dreams is not going to help us to know who we are. And it is knowing who we are that is at issue when it comes to the true universal law of attraction. In order to take this journey with the gentleness, self-compassion and respect required, we are going to have to put aside some faulty views of the shadow.

The shadow is not simply the receptacle for all the trash in our lives, which we have failed to take out to the street for pick-up. It is not a deep dark force for evil. It is not simply a place for repressed memories of childhood abuse. It is not just the home of everything opposite to what we want and need in life. Nor is it an exact replica of the ego, in its darkest or inferior form. The shadow is dark only because the solid objectification of ourselves as flesh, blood and bone is blocking us from the light of our own souls. The shadow is simply a storage place for everything we do not know about ourselves—both collectively and individually. *Everything* we do not know about ourselves is hidden in the shadow.

The reason that it has been so easy for us to dilute and distort the true nature of the shadow is that we all have inherited an archetypal image of ourselves as basically evil at the core. We will speak more about why this is true in a later chapter, but for now what we need to know is that for centuries our idea has been that because we are intrinsically "bad" we were going to have to *force* ourselves to be better people by striving after "goodness," doing the "right" thing, and learning to be morally incorruptible. In order to do that we were going to have to fight against our natural selves—the natural man—the ungodly truth of who we really are. We were put here, we supposed, in order to outsmart our basically "evil" impulses. And in order to do that, we were going to have to use the only power we thought we had—repression.

Though we have managed to change our thinking dramatically in many other areas of our lives, even the most secular among us still very often, at least unconsciously, hold to these ideas.

A man who lives as a hit-man for the Mafia, for example, may become embarrassed and apologize for using curse words in front of a nun. She serves as a reminder to him that he is not living a "good" life, even though his last hit didn't remind him of that at all. A child who cheats on her exam at school, though no one else punishes her, may need to find a way to harshly punish herself for her "badness." A woman who is otherwise very "good" in the classic sense of the word, will be ruthlessly self-critical when she has a thought of revenge because her obnoxious boss raked her over the coals for something she didn't do. These are all examples of our fear that at base, we are really just bad to the bone. The only thing that seems to keep us from totally living out our erasable "badness" is the fact that we are ever striving to be "good" people.

The evidence of our evil nature seems to be all around us, ranging from the massive genocides of current and historic horror, to the lies we tell our bosses about being late to a meeting. And in order to keep ourselves from sinking all the way down to those most atrocious evils, we have to constantly stay on top of ourselves. And so we live lives of duty, and obligation and we create laws and institutions that are meant to keep us on the straight and narrow. If we didn't do that, we are certain that we would become the monsters lurking around in our shadows. And if we are not the monster—someone else surely is—for there definitely *is* a monster.

Being a "good" person satisfies that little child within us who wants to make sure he doesn't get "in trouble." And we assume that such "goodness" should get us all the magical rewards due to us—a good marriage, good children and a fulfilling career life—because after all, we are "good" people. This is why, when something "bad" happens to us, our first cry is "fowl!" "It isn't fair" we say, stomping our little feet and swearing that we didn't deserve this!

And this is why the current understanding of the law of attraction is so appealing to so many people. It offers an explanation for the seemingly unfair events in our lives: We attracted them through "negative" thinking. But this understanding of the law of attraction only perpetuates the problem in which we think that we have to deserve a good life—a problem that makes it so much harder for us to accept life on Life's terms. The magical thinking of "just rewards" is the bargain we make that keeps us from such acceptance.

But when we are shocked by a reality that doesn't fit our schema, we don't throw out the magical thinking. No! We try to figure out what it is that we can do to fit this new life event into that old paradigm. Enter the current understanding of the law of attraction, which informs us that this event happened because we are manifesting our "negative" thoughts and all we need to do now is think "positive" thoughts and the topsy-turvy world will be turned aright again. And off we go. So it is, that this archetypal idea of ourselves as basically "bad" people having to work at being "good" gets in the way of our ability to see the shadow for exactly what it is— a neutral place in the psyche that holds everything that we do not know about ourselves.

If this is true, we might want to start considering what kinds of things we don't know about ourselves. Let's use the same schema above to illustrate the nature of these unknowns. Because the collective humanity has consciously perpetuated this mythology of a grand battle between "good" and "evil," what lies underneath that masking motif has great depth and height. So, on the conscious level there is this eternal battle, but what lives in the shadow, unknown to us and awaiting our realization, is the fact that "good" and "evil" are but labels we have used to help us live in a world we don't want to accept.

We can see this fact clearly when we consider the inmate in a prison who sneaks to do "good" in the same way that others sneak to do "bad." He has identified with "badness" for so long that it is frightening for him to consider being "good." In his shadow then, will be found all of that "goodness" he's been repressing. Of course, not only does this mean that the shadow is not a receptacle for "evil," but it also means that he's really not "bad" after all, when you consider him as more than the sum total of his visible behavior. If we could consider him to be a human who is struggling in his own ineffective way with the potential for suffering, then we don't have to ask if he is "good" or "evil" but can pull from our own shadows the realization that those terms serve no other purpose than to help *us* cope with *our* fears.

How many times have we been extremely angry at someone for some perceived "evil" only to later learn that this person was struggling with some unbelievable burden, so that we were then able to let it go without further recrimination? How were we able to do that? Well, we might say that we found out that the person wasn't "evil" after all, and yes, so we did; but then we might find that out about everyone if we stopped to get to know them. This kind of wise acceptance, once it rises to the surface, makes us proud to be human beings. And if we were able to unbury it from its place deep in the collective shadow, we might, indeed, change our world.

While it is true that we can look around the world and see suffering, and while it is true that some of that suffering is a result of the actions of people who deliberately set about to harm others, does this necessarily mean that those people were evil? Because we have "good" and "evil" as the imprintable cultural options from which we, as very young and forming psyches, may choose to identify, some, who feel they must, will choose so-called "evil" as the safest option. But if these concepts were not imprinted on the psyche at such tender ages, even passed down as archetypes, then perhaps we could stop identifying with them! So, as long as we continue to consciously split-off our understanding of life into these two indefinable but ever-broadening categories, we will continue to perpetuate these mythologies and our children will continue to identify with them. But in the shadow exists an entirely different paradigm, one that not only does not use that limp terminology, but one that recognizes the potential power in each human psyche.

From that perspective then, as we look into the shadow, we find insights we could never have found if we just continued to accept the old paradigm. In fact, there is nothing that can be found in the shadow that does not have a unique treasure attached to it. When, for example, I uncover anger I might find at its roots, all of my needs to protect and bring forth into conscious awareness the Self. If I uncover intense repressed fear, I could also find my own sacred vulnerability. And if I live in a world in which *Being* is not supported, but *doing* is the primary way to gain respect from the world (i.e., the world in which we all live); then Beingness is going to be found in the shadow. We are unconscious of this Beingness, the I AM nature, because we have consciously identified with the ID we discussed in Chapter 5.

What we will discover then is that everything that is buried in the shadow has in fact been placed in fertile soil intended to grow our awareness of Divine Self, which is actually rooted there in the shadow. So, when we think of "clearing shadow blocks," we might want to think again, for these so-called "blocks" could be constituent energetic parts of the wholeness that is Self. We simply do not need to run too fast and loose into this amazing Ultimacy called the shadow. But we can, if we go slowly, gently and with respect for its mystery and force, learn to both receive it and live on the energy we find there.

How can we do that? We begin by understanding that there is absolutely no elemental energy within us that is not supported, even underscored by the Self. This means that nothing, absolutely nothing exists beyond Divine Self. It means that every emotion, every thought, every behavior, every belief, everything within us has a Divine root system. That does *not* mean that every thought or feeling, etc., is correct, accurate or effective. It means that at base, the soul's root system is pushing everything else in our lives toward Divine awareness.

We've already seen that sitting with our emotions is how we access the energy behind them. We learn from them of our vulnerable, soft underbelly; we learn where there is a problem that needs a resolution; we learn about the things we love and the things we don't like so much—information which gives us direction if we let it. We learn about ourselves. But if we take that one step deeper and don't just say that we learn about ourselves from the perspective of a personality, but also from the perspective of our own Divine nature, then we can begin to access the emotion's Divine source.

If I sit with the emotion of fear, for example, and listen to what it is telling me, I will not only find my own sweet vulnerability, but I will also find a raw, potent and mysterious energy. We might say that the emotion I recognize as fear is but the tip of the iceberg. Below that tip, deep in the waters of the unconscious, I will find an enormous power—a power that is a constituent part of the wholeness I AM. What then will I do with that power? Suppose that I am afraid of running out of money before the end of the month. If I sit with that fear and just objectively listen to its message, not really buying it, just listening; I am likely to not only hear its urgent plea for help, but I might just come up with some ideas about how to get more money for those last few days before the end of the month. Already I've tapped into something of my internal leadership. But once I have listened for a while longer, I might begin to feel something beneath the fear, something that is not talking about money or time, but about a gentle unswerving knowing. This knowing carries a kind of energy or feeling that communicates "it's going to be okay," or it may just feel like "sit down and be still." But it is the fear that brought me to that place of knowing. Now that I am aware of that knowing, I might learn to access it, at least some of the time, without having to go to fear first.

Sometimes this works with physical pain as well. If you have aching muscles or joints you might want to try this. As you slip down into yourself during meditation, feel that pain. Just sit with it and feel it. Feel its colors, its smells; see what it might look like and just be still. Now imagine going down under the pain. What is beneath it? What does that feel like? What are its colors, shapes, sounds and meanings? Upon answering some of these questions, you might notice that at first the pain goes away as you focus on the energy behind it. But the minute you remove your focus from the energy behind it, the pain comes back. As you get more and more practiced with focusing on what is beneath the pain, you are beginning to access the Divine Self.

The Divine Self or soul has never been wounded. It is wise and loving. It has enormous compassion for us. It is a very active potent force, which cannot be contained or stopped. It is a constant in our lives, though we don't often know it. And if we get down to the bottom line of what it is we truly want in life—it is a deep and abiding association with this energetic, active, powerful, beautiful and peaceful presence of Self within. We want to experience being right up next to it, cozy under its armpit, even inside it. And once we've had a real taste, a real solid glimpse of what the Divine Self feels, acts, thinks, walks and emotes like, we want nothing else.

Here's how the Gospel of Philip puts it:

> 6Light and darkness, life and death, right and left, are brothers of each other.[13] It is not possible to separate them from each other. So, those who are good are not good, those who are evil are not evil, nor is life really life, nor death really death.[14] Thus each shall be dissolved into what it was at the beginning (Smith 2005, 13).*

As we sit with these deeper regions of ourselves we are beginning to dissolve into our earliest origin. But if instead, we tell ourselves that we are not supposed to have these so-called "negative" emotions, or any physical pain because these are evidence that we haven't quite got the law of attraction down yet, then we are denying ourselves the gift that these emotions and sensations came to give us. Further, we are missing the one and only thing we truly desire—the Self.

Now all of those who espouse the current understanding of the law of attraction are, right about now, screaming, "But does this mean that I can't have my dreams?" Once we get it that we *are* actually Divine Self, then that Self takes over the driver's seat. It will then create itself again and anew in the life. But, let's be very clear here. We do not attain to such knowledge lightly. So, if we are thinking "Okay, now let me get busy trying to find my Divine Self so that I can have all these other things I want," we are still missing the point. The point, the only point is the Divine Self, Ultimate Consciousness, the soul. The ***real*** law of attraction is this: *We are attracted to and by those situations, persons, places, things, etc. which will bring us clearly and essentially to the power of Ultimate Consciousness of Divine Self.*

And now that we know that, let's discover what other Universal laws are working with the real law of attraction to help that process along.

* Excerpt is from *The Gospel of Philip: Annotated & Explained,* 2005 by Andrew Phillip Smith. Permission granted by SkyLight Paths Publishing, Woodstock, VT, www.skylightpaths.com.

8

Mutual Reciprocity

The *true* law of attraction does not operate in a vacuum. In fact, it operates in collaboration with other *equally powerful* laws. Where there appears to be disharmony between these laws, in actuality each is utilizing the energy of the other to accomplish its task in much the same way that the law of motion factors the law of gravity into its equation. Like the physical laws of the Universe, these laws cannot be created or destroyed. They simply are. And though we may choose to operate as if they don't exist, they do exist and they continue to operate in our lives regardless of our attention to them. The following discussion will explain these laws and how they interact with the law of attraction.

The Law of Projection

On the flip side of the law of attraction coin is the law of projection. With the true law of attraction we are attracted to and by those situations, places, persons and things, etc., which will bring us inexorably to Ultimate Consciousness of the Divine Self. With the law of projection we not only repress information we do not wish to know about ourselves, but we also project this information outward onto other people, places, things and circumstances. The initial intent is to resist becoming conscious. It works like this: First, there is a particular truth that I do not wish to know about myself, so I repress it. But every now and then that energy is going to need expression. Still, I cannot let it express lest I become aware of it. So, I project it. I send it out onto people that I know or people that I don't know.

For example, let's say I'm a gay man named Gary, and I'm in denial. I've been raised in a strict religious discipline that has taught me that gays, lesbians, bisexuals and transgendered persons are actually very sinful and are just using others for their perversions. Some part of me doesn't really believe this, but accepting that scares me to death, because I'm certain that everyone I love will be lost to me if I am true to myself. As I grow up I avoid living out my most genuine sexual orientation by repressing that energy. Every time I become even slightly aware of it, I become nervous and angry. But instead of using that agitation as awareness, I project it outward, assuming that others are agitated with me. So, I grow a chip on my shoulder. As I evolve into sexuality and romance, I have to work harder and harder to repress, and find it easier and easier to project outward. Since most people I know equate masculinity with heterosexuality, I not only become a Police Officer to prove my masculinity, but on the job I am hypervigilant about being seen as masculine. I deliberately act anti-gay. I may even carry it to the extreme of bashing gays—since I'm projecting my agitation as well. For example, I might stalk men coming out of gay bars and use every opportunity I can think of to arrest them.

Why would I do that? Because I have arrested my own very natural development as a gay man. Of course, being gay isn't a sin or a perversion. In fact, it is not about sex per se. Being gay means I *fall in love* with people of the same gender. It isn't called homo-*sex*-uality, because it is about sex. It is called homo-*sex*-uality because it is about *gender*—the gender with whom one typically falls in love. If we could just let ourselves admit it, falling in love is a sacred and spiritual act regardless of who we fall in love with or what happens after that.

But if I am Gary, I can't think these things, because they make me feel as if I'll lose those I love, and it will, at least for a while, make me wonder about my worth as a person. So, I'll continue to project it onto others, and act as if they need to question their worth and they need to be separated from the people they love. They'll get the punishment I think that I might just deserve. And the more disgusted I appear to be with all of those others who are gay, the more disgusted I really am with myself. This is how projection works. It keeps me from having to deal with my own issues.

I made this case deliberately overt for the purpose of clarity. But it can definitely be much more subtle. One example from my own life occurred when I'd taken on an Interim position as a Program Director while I was also holding down a position as a Family Therapist in the same organization. I had so many balls to juggle that I'd become quite disorganized and frazzled internally, while I came across as "oh so together" on the outside. I had a counselor who was working for me at that time whose disorganization and seeming laziness just irritated me to death. So much so in fact, that I began to dread our weekly meetings just because I couldn't stand to be in the room with him.

When I realized my completely irrational reaction to him I began to ask myself why I felt this way. I looked at the similarities and differences between us, and to the metaphors relative to the stories we told about our work. I found that the reason I so disliked him was because I was calling myself lazy for not being able to keep up with the enormity of tasks in a given day, and I was, because of this self-judgment and its projection, unable to actually get down to the business of organizing my day.

So, I pulled back the projection and put the energy where it belonged—on me. I began to see that I was not lazy at all, but that this was a term my mother used frequently to judge her children and others. In fact, I was overwhelmed. And I needed to get a grip. So, I decided to make a list of my tasks and ask myself which of these tasks I really enjoyed the most and which I enjoyed less and then less, and I prioritized accordingly. I began to feel that I was much more in control of my workload because after doing the things that I loved first, I had energy to do the things I liked less later. And I developed a let-it-go attitude toward the things I didn't get to today, knowing they'd still be there tomorrow. And guess what? I started liking my supervisee again. In fact, after that, without my having to say a word, he began to get more organized and efficient in his work so that he was free to focus better on client care. And this is the law of projection in action: Not only do we keep ourselves from solving problems effectively by projecting, but others can literally pick that energy up and carry it for us.

It works exactly the same on the collective level. For example, for centuries the darker races have carried, for the Caucasian race, fear of powerlessness and its affiliate shame. What happened as a result of that projection and the ensuing treatment white America gave to Africans and then African Americans is that many of them actually picked up and carried that shame and powerlessness, as if they had something of which to be ashamed and as if they had no personal power. That combination has trapped many African Americans in poverty and all that comes with it. But as they began to realize their own power, we began to feel ashamed of ourselves for how we had treated them and they began to remove those shackles. We all have yet more work to do in this department, but neither black nor white America will ever be able to fully move beyond projected Caucasian fear of powerlessness and shame until Caucasians can pull that projection back, own it and heal it.

Also on a collective level, we of the Western world have projected abject poverty and starvation on to the previously so-called third world countries. The term *third world*, now considered to be politically incorrect, once had the ability to create psychic distance between "us" and "them." They were not just another country to us. They were a whole other world, and not just a second world, but a third world. But though we've virtually done away with the term, yet the psychic distance remains. "Over there" there is poverty and starvation and genocide. But "over here" we don't have those things. Over here in the Western world, we have decided that we will not allow our fear of abject poverty and starvation into our psychic awareness. We strive after money as the primary goal in life and grow more and more obese. We rarely-to-never have media light shown on the starvation that is happening right here in America or in other Western countries, because we just don't want to think about that.

So, we project that onto a "they" "out there," while refusing to realize that "they" are us. In the West there are billions of dollars every day going to cars, food, clothes, churches, homes, movies, businesses, bonuses, credit cards, etc. Think of the millions of dollars it takes to make a single Hollywood movie. Think of the millions that movie takes in over a single weekend, as it goes to the theatres. All of that is happening every day while we ignore the poverty "over there," where simultaneously, starvation is occurring daily.

Poverty and starvation do not have to occur in these countries. In fact, if we took even a small portion of the money that exchanges hands here every day and put it into feeding that other part of our Oneness, there would be no starvation. Anywhere. But we don't want to do that. We want to keep the specter of starvation away from the doors to our conscious awareness by holding on to our money. We just won't let ourselves think about it.

The best we do in most cases is warn our children that they should eat what's on their plates because of the starving children in whatever country onto which we've projected the worst of our fears. So, now what have we done? We have passed down to our children our need to project those fears outward. Now they too will eat more for the starving children they will never see or talk to and stuff their fear of starvation and poverty down into the back closets of their psyches. Later, we will send a token guilt offering to feed the starving children in another country and brush it off our hands.

Some of us use greed to keep starvation fears at bay. And some of us sacrifice our own happiness in some kind of survivor's guilt, by refusing to pursue the careers and avocations to which our souls call us, because there are unhappy people in the world. "Why should I be happy when so many others are suffering," we ask. Of course, the answer is that our happiness and their suffering are One. Does this mean that, instead of opting for greed or guilt, every one of us should be working in some developing nation to rid the world of poverty?

Well, no, but yes. There are no shoulds, but if I were to make a recommendation here it would be this: We can pull back our fears, own them, address them as real and recognize that our fear is part of our calling to empathy. If we all admitted to ourselves that we have a deep-seated fear of starvation and began to address that fear directly, we would automatically be pulling back and owning our projections about it. This means that what used to be called third world would become first world in our psyches and the wealth of the Western world would automatically become available to those in this new first world.

The most amazing feature of this projection, however, is that while we are over here on occasion feeling sorry for the poor starving children over there, we don't realize that it is we who are poor. They are carrying the energy of our projection for us by agreeing with us that the problem is money—which, of course, it absolutely is not. They live out our fears for us every single day, out of a soul-level love that we can't even imagine while they simultaneously project onto us their own personal and collective power. We gladly take the power from them, and somewhere deep in their souls, they gladly take the poverty for us. We will have more to say about the riches of this kind of love later, but for now, suffice it to say that it's difficult to know who is the poorest.

The law of projection works with the law of attraction as follows. Our false identities tend to consistently look for mirrors. And we want mirrors that reflect only what we think we know about ourselves. So, using the law of attraction, we imagine those people onto whom we can project those things we don't want to know about ourselves and then set about the process of avoiding them, in the same way that we avoided the material we repressed in the first place. These people populate our worlds, whether these are imaginary or real worlds, and they have just enough of the look of what we want to project to make us believe that our projection fits. They look like a duck, quack like a duck, walk like a duck...you know what? I think it's a duck. But deep down inside we are quacking like hell. And yet, because of the law of attraction we often cannot avoid the emotional impact of these people, or the places and things that carry our projections, even if we manage to avoid them physically. Thus the projection itself gives us yet another opportunity to become conscious, bringing us just that much closer to wholeness.

The Law of One

The reason that both the law of projection and the true law of attraction work so effectively is because all is One. In fact, the reason all of the Universal laws work is because they work in conjunction and harmony with the law of One. The reason that a psychic can see what he or she sees is because we are all One. Yeah, that takes a little of the woo-woo out of it, doesn't it? The reason that I knew my sister had been in an automobile accident and was possibly dead, even though I was miles away in my home reading a college lit assignment, is because she and I are One. But I am not just One with my loved ones. I am One with all the serial killers and masters of genocide as well. And so are we all.

But even that does not tell the whole story. We are also One with all the objects, animals, plants and elements on the planet. This does not mean that we, as the great and supreme humans, are dominating all of those things—as we've been taught in some of our religious traditions. It means we are equally a part of every other energy on the planet. Those energies impact us and we equally impact them. However, this might mean that we need to reconsider the source of such "acts of God" as earthquakes, tornadoes and hurricanes. Oneness means that our collective energies have some say-so about what is going on here.

But even that does not say it all. We are also One with all the other energies in the Universe. Gravity for example, and the laws of motion, the laws of conservation, thermodynamic laws, laws of gases, and quantum laws. We are One with all of those and more. We are One with all the other planets in the Universe. This is why astrology can be trusted—when it's done well and fully—because we are One with the planetary energies and we can find out what impact we are having on the planets and the planets are having on us.

Oneness also means that we are One with ourselves. The body is not split-off and separate from the soul. Though, down through the ages, we have blamed "the flesh" for all manner of "evil" and have decided, therefore, that the way to "goodness" is to pay no attention to the body or worse, to beat it into submission. According to that belief, when we die, we are at last free of that nasty encumbrance and we can finally get to our souls. But the law of One says that our bodies are *already* One with our souls.

The mind is not split-off from the soul either. But because we think that it is, we believe that we must control our thoughts to push them into "positive thinking," as we imagine that the soul must match our own connotation of the word *positive*. It is this belief that perpetuates our current understanding of the law of attraction. But if the mind is not really split-off but only thinks that it is, then it can be aligned with the soul, simply through the recognition of that simple truth.

And one more thing: We are One with the Divine. We, therefore, have and can own all the power of omnipotence, omnipresence, and omniscience, the power of unconditional love, the power of health, the power of eternity and infinity. We can say, as the Divine says in the text quoted previously: "The cattle on a thousand hills are mine." And just so, we belong to the cattle on a thousand hills, and those cattle are also Divine Beings.

So why don't we know this? Well, that would be because of the next law.

The Law of Duality

We are here on a mission. A mission assigned to us in the metaphorical Garden of Eden, when we were given two options: The option of living in the knowledge of "good" and "evil," and the option of living in Life. The Life option was the one in which we could remain fully aware of our Oneness with all things and with the Divine. But because we did not choose this option, it has now become the river of Life that flows beneath everything else in our lives informing and energizing every aspect of our being, mostly without our knowledge. The option of knowledge of "good" and "evil" is the trance state of duality in which we all collectively chose to live.

We chose this and hypnotized ourselves into that trance state because it was ours to choose; because as One with the Divine we are constantly co-creating the Universe. Creation occurs continuously as a process of both acceptance and elimination. If I am painting a picture, as I paint I am choosing what colors to use, what strokes and what designs. This means I am also choosing what colors I won't use, and what strokes and what designs. Just so, the creative process invites *all* options with regard to what will and will not be created. So, as we were painting life on planet earth, the question arose: Does living in matter or form separate us from the formless Divine? This was a natural question to ask as a part of the creative process—and one that was fully a part of Divine intention.

It was our co-creative intention with the Divine that planet earth should be the place in the Universe in which form is realized as One with formlessness. In order to bring about that intention, we were going to have to *fully experience* the other option. Just as a painter might have to paint purple into the picture and then stand back to look at it, before he can realize that green is the truer color; we were going to have to fully experience duality before we could realize Oneness as form. In any creative endeavor, *all* possibilities are extant until the creation is complete. So, rather than staying in full consciousness of Life, in which we knew ourselves to be Divine, we agreed to fall into a trance state in which we could fully experience a life of separation from the Divine. Through that trance state we have created a world in which duality—or that notion of our separation from the Divine—is fully lived out. This means that not only do we believe ourselves separate from the Divine, but we have created a world in which everything and everyone appears to also be separate from us. We are doing all of this in order to fully experience every road, and explore every avenue of duality. This journey must be an experiential enterprise, for the fundamental question of our own essential nature cannot be answered through mere intellectual endeavor.

Ultimately these experiences will bring us to the answer to our original question. But of course, once we have run to the end of every experiential road, what we will finally remember is that we have not been nor could we ever be separate from the Divine—for our very form is Divine. We will awaken from the trance state, having fully experienced the other option to Oneness and put it completely to rest. And once we as a collective have experientially determined that duality is unfounded, the entire Universe—with which we are One—will be alchemically transformed in such a way that form and formlessness will be realized as One throughout the entire Universe. Once Divine energy was "formless and void" (Genesis 1:2), but in the end the Divine will encompass both the formless and the formed, and the creation we understand as form will finally be complete. The painting of form will finally be finished. Forever after this journey is over, Oneness will be a done deal.

Our mission then, here on planet earth is to give that gift of tested, qualified Oneness as form to the Universe.

This is, indeed, a brave journey we are taking. One in which once we are here and have identified with our lives here, we actually believe that the Divine is far away from us. But because that idea is too hard to bear we created the mythology that we could at least earn the right to be close or semi-close to the Divine by being "good," because it must have been our "badness" that drove the Divine away in the first place. On this journey and because of that mythology, we suffer; we stumble around in the darkness of the duality trance state trying to find some kind of meaning in life. But the amazing thing is that regardless of how dark that blindness has become, we still find a reason to live. We still find joy, we still give great gifts of love, brilliance and heroism to each other, and we still find life to be poignant and rich. This alone is evidence that something else is going on here.

We have determined, however, that what happened in the metaphorical Garden of Eden was a huge mistake. A sin, in fact. Because that choice has allowed us to experience the suffering inherent to the duality trance state, we assume that the suffering is some kind of punishment or at least the consequence of our choice—which makes that choice a sin. We have always equated our suffering with evil or wrongness. But our suffering is actually a constituent part of the duality trance state, which declares that we are separate from the Divine and therefore, separate from abundant supply, love, peace, joy and even parts of ourselves.

Here we come to the nature of the law of duality that acts in concert with the law of One. Though duality gives us the power to live *as if* we were separate from the Divine, it is not really possible for us to be separated from anything, especially the Divine, for all is One. In fact, Eden still lives within us. It is the place within, in which we know constant abundant supply, and are consumed with the knowledge of who we are as Divine

Beings. We, like Jesus, can absolutely say, "I and the Father are One" (John 10:30). And yet, we have so hypnotized ourselves into the duality trance state that we think making such a claim is either blasphemous or utterly ridiculous.

The river of Life that flows beneath every single thought, feeling, belief and action is actually the owner of every aspect of our lives. But because we chose to live in the trance state of duality before we came here, we believe that life is short, that we must hurry to accomplish our life tasks and that there are things that are beyond our grasp that we must work hard to attract by means that include thought control. The truth is, however, that we can't die. No one dies. Life is eternal. And we don't have to attract anything. It is already ours. Yet, we, as a collective are still living in the mindset of duality.

But the *real* law of attraction actually works in harmony with the law of duality and the law of One, by attracting those things, situations and people that nudge us ultimately toward the truth that form and formlessness are One. All we need to do to become aware of the work of the law of attraction is to look around at the situations, people, places and things in our lives and *see,* really see how they are leading us closer to our truest nature.

The Law of Visibility and Invisibility

What we see is everything. Simply everything. We create, manage and maintain our lives based on what we see—except that all those things we don't see still have power and capacity to create, manage and maintain our lives. This is the basic overview of the law of visibility and invisibility. What it means ultimately is that the law is completely fulfilled when we raise our consciousness so that we see all those things that were previously invisible to us.

The completion of our job here on planet earth will be to become fully conscious. We are meant to become fully aware of our bodies, our hearts, our minds, and our souls as One. This is our ultimate destiny. And so as we are processing through our blindness, we can take comfort in the fact that our blindness is just one side of the coin that is our Oneness with ourselves.

Quite often I have clients who are struggling with regret over not having seen something earlier. The spouse was cheating and they didn't see it. They married an abusive person and missed the early signs. They committed to someone for whom they didn't have real love, out of a deep need for security or something like it and they didn't see this, and so stayed married for years. They look back on their blindness filled with regret and a sense of real loss. And they are beating themselves up for not seeing sooner.

My response to this is: "You can't see what you don't see until you see it." And that is a part of the law of visibility and invisibility. It's the law. And not seeing is just as much a part of our process here on planet earth as is seeing. If the previously discussed law of duality is true, then our journey into blindness is just as important as our journey into seeing. Indeed, the more we see of separation, the closer we come to seeing unity. The more we see of powerlessness, the more we are coming into consciousness of complete power. We are gaining information and experience with every encounter with the world we are creating. We absolutely must transition through periods or even lives of blindness, in order to fully experience that blindness. And once we have fully experienced blindness, we will begin to see. And because we have gone through the entire experience, we will have grown in ways that cannot even be put into words, once we arrive at the other side.

This law interacts with the law of attraction in this way: We are attracted to what we cannot see in order to come to see it. How long it takes us to see it is part of the experience, part of the journey into seeing. There are deep inner excursions we can take into our hearts and minds simply *because* we cannot see. In other words, there is a seeing that only blindness can offer us.

When we reduce this beautiful law, to thought control, we have missed the point of our journey completely. However, this does not mean that we cannot enhance our journey by going within to see. In fact, the more we hear from our souls, the more open we become to real seeing. The more we practice fulfilling our truest soul desires, the more we open to deeper desires. The more we hear the more we listen. The more we see, the more there is to see. This is the law of visibility and invisibility.

The Law of Choice

The choice to live on planet earth in the trance state of duality has already been made. Because that is true, from birth we have all been looking to get someone or something to tell us who we are. We look for mirrors everywhere. And what we see is people who tell us that we are separate from the Divine. But the soul, the authentic Self knows who we are, and so we also have a choice to begin to live out who we really are. We have the choice to develop our consciousness to the degree that there is no doubt whatsoever who we are. The choice to awaken is given to us all day every day. We may awaken to each moment, or not, as we choose.

Sometimes in my practice, I treat a person who has begun to consider the possibility of suicide. One of the most effective interventions I have found thus far in working with these individuals is to remind them that they've had the choice to kill themselves all day every day since the day they were born, but for some reason, they haven't done it. It is paradoxical, but the effect of this realization is that the person begins to take conscious responsibility for the power to choose—which in turn makes it more feasible to stay long enough to see if he or she can work out the current problem. So far, I haven't had a single client commit suicide. But that's not because I'm keeping them alive—regardless of my training, I simply don't have the power to make someone else's choices for them. Each person came here to experience his or her own journey. And that journey is a constituent and essential part of the journey we all are taking as a collective. So, if they are still here, it is because they chose to stick this incarnation out.

That same paradox is true of awakening. We have the choice all day every day to open up to awareness of who we really are. And the moment we turn to look in the mirror of our souls we will get as much light as we allow in. This is the law of choice. And law of attraction interacts with it by bringing us mirrors of the soul into which we may look. Of course, if we choose we may also look for the mirrors of identification with duality in order to continue to see the same old thing. But that's the law of choice.

We resist accepting this law more than any other. We fear that if we realize that we've always had a choice, then we must blame ourselves for our circumstances. But choice is not synonymous with blame. In fact, choice happens frequently on subliminal levels of which we are not even aware. I saw this again just the other day when I dropped two different things. One of those things was very important, even sacred to me. So, when I felt it falling, I chose not to let it fall all the way to the ground. And my grasp was as quick and silent as that choice. As I captured it back in my hands again I was very aware that I'd just been deep within myself. From that place deep within, I heard the choice not to let it fall happening so quickly that on another day, in another frame of mind, I would not have even noticed it.

Later in the same day I dropped my car keys, but they fell to the ground before I caught them. And from that same deep place I noted that something in me chose to let them go, just as quickly as earlier I'd chosen not to let the sacred object fall. It didn't matter if my keys fell. I could just scoop them back up again. But if the sacred object had fallen it would have broken, and I just was not going to allow that to happen. In both cases I was there, deep inside of me, hearing myself make that quicker-than-a-nanosecond choice. It was quite enlightening.

First, we actually can become so acquainted with the inner terrain that we can feel these faster-than-the-speed-of-light choices, actions, reactions and responses occurring. I think that if I really worked at it, I could remember the choices I made to drop the sacred object and the keys in the first place. But these choices usually occur on a subliminal or even unconscious level. Yet they do occur. And they demonstrate that we are much more in charge than we think. While this reality makes it clear that we are not the helpless victims of random forces operating beyond our grasp, it still terrifies us. We want and we don't want to know that we have a choice. But if it is true that we are in charge of these moment-to-moment choices, then it seems apparent that we need to be very much in touch with these moments—which brings us to the next law.

The Law of Now

Currently, Western pop psychology seems to be all about deciding what damaging effects our past has had on us, and what we can do to move beyond the past into the future. Of course, there is not much room in there for the present. But the law of now is a fact. There is no past and there is no future. There is always only now.

Time does not exist in the law of now. Time is a creation of duality thinking. While time does allow us to mark events, it also implies that there is a limit. There are no limits and there is no time. Well, we could argue, the day ends and night comes and we have to sleep. But the law of now says that there is always plenty of timelessness. In the world in which the law of now is in complete control we are not concerned about time at all, for all is now. Now we already have and are everything, for all is now One. Now we are living into all the relationships and encounters and circumstances that are essential for our awakening into now. The past cannot damage us, because there is no past. The future is not something we strive toward, because there is no future.

If we are so awake we take in each breath of nowness fully aware of both the internal and the external of that now. Colors are brighter, because we really see them, smells are stronger because we are alive to them, sounds resonate in the marrow of the bones, thoughts and emotions are round and full. The law of attraction works in harmony with the law of now in that we are attracted to and by our own awakening to the now. This means that every life event, person, place or thing in our lives right now has been attracted by and to that awakening.

The most interesting thing about the law of now is that it is always occurring. But for most of us it occurs on another level of consciousness. This means that while we are unaware of it, there is always a place deep within us that is operating out of this law. It is not striving for the future, or seeking to attract something it does not yet own, for it knows that all is already ours. And the more conscious we are of the now, the more apt we are to be aware of the action of the law of attraction in our lives. But that will also work in collaboration with the next law:

The Law of Karma

Typically we see karma as a function of duality. We did something in a past life for which in the next life we need punishment or, as it is euphemistically called, "balancing." But from the perspective of the law of karma in harmony with all the other Universal laws, karma is simply the *intention* to awaken. With each incarnation we come closer and closer to our truest soul Self. The ultimate intention is for soul to merge with mind and body in our conscious awareness so that we live in the body and mind as soul. The energy that pushes this process is karma, the deep and powerful intention within each individual and within all of us as a collective.

In our current duality trance state, however, we believe that the soul is outside the body, separate and opposite from it. In fact, the very thought of body and soul as One is almost ludicrous to traditional thought. Body is for earth; soul is for heaven. It is really a head-trip for most of us to consider this any other way. But the law of karma is the soul's intention for form to realize Oneness with formlessness. According to the law of One, the body doesn't separate us from our Divine nature—it is just as much a part of our Divine nature as is our spirituality. But according to the law of duality, we are currently experiencing the body as separate from the soul or the Divine nature. The law of karma is the intention that moves us through the process of the duality trance state by slowly raising our consciousness from one incarnation to the next, to the place in which we fully embrace and encapsulate the soul within the body and the body within the soul.

Karma is the intention that the mind begin to think the thoughts of the soul and the heart begin to feel the emotions of the soul. But currently the duality trance state has us believing that we cannot think and feel like a soul until we are dead. Again, wrapping our minds around the possibility that we can think Divine or soul thoughts and feel Divine or soul feelings is extremely difficult for us, so entranced have we become with the duality mindset—which has become our traditional thinking. But it was, we might imagine, equally hard for Galileo, that great master thinker of the fifteenth century, to recognize that the earth revolved around the sun, instead of the sun revolving around the earth as had been thought for eons. And yet, it was true.

Karma is not the energy of pay back, or what comes around goes around, or the energy of balancing one life's inequities with another life's equities. We are not poor in this life, because we were rich in another and gave nothing to the poor. We are not poor in this life because we were poor in the last and that is our caste. We are poor in this life because we are seeking knowledge of "good" and "evil"—as it is put in the Bible—we are seeking to fully know and understand duality so that we can finally put it to rest. We are poor in this life because we have come here to experience poverty—whether we stay in it or not—so that we will know it and reach its ultimate conclusion: Oneness. The karma in such poverty is but the intention that we reach that ultimate conclusion.

As we live the life of each incarnation, we take on more and more information and experience that informs the split-off mind that we are actually One. The ego and the shadow are meant to become One with the soul or Divine nature. But it is the split between the ego and the shadow that keeps us unaware of all of the other splits. Once we agreed to participate in the duality trance state, we created a secret place to hide Oneness from conscious experience. As we've said, that place is the shadow. And, because our truest identity was then unconscious to us, the ego developed ego-states. So now, the division is almost automatic. Whatever the ego does not want to assimilate goes into the shadow. And whatever it accepts goes to identity like packing fists full of snow onto a snowman. But as the centuries pass and we experience one incarnation after another, because the soul intends it, we are coming closer and closer to direct knowledge of who we really are. As that process continues the chasm between the ego and the shadow begins to close.

Now in the twenty-first century we are beginning to allow the ego to explore the shadow a bit. More and more of us are becoming aware of other levels of existence than those to which we have attached ourselves as a collective. Just as technology has revved up and surpassed our previous understanding of communication, distance, and speed, so our psychology is now revving up to allow us more capacity for deeper levels of awareness and more understanding of who we are. But these things are all happening on the basis of *experience*. We must experience our experiments with technology and medicine in order to come to new places with them. And the same is true with the trance state of duality. We must experience it, and experiment with different aspects of it in order to move beyond it. The intention that is karma utilizes the experiences brought to us by the law of attraction to bring us to greater and deeper levels of evolution and transformation.

Currently, however, because of our duality trance state, most of us still believe that we can harm one another and ourselves, that the past can damage us, that some people can be rich and others poor, and that our bodies can betray us through illness. And we live out those beliefs entirely. But as we experience these things again and again through one incarnation after another, some of us have begun to learn about the deeper planes of experience; we've begun to wonder if the dualistic plane of experience is really truth. As we continue to experiment with this over lifetimes, we will come closer and closer to ourselves. We will reach down ever deeper into the hidden aspects of our beings and find more and more of our power, our Oneness and our Divinity. Because these are the ultimate truths, there is absolutely no way that our experimental and creative journey into duality can fail to bring us to the ultimacy of our essence. The reason this is so is that there is a Divine intention, barely understood on the earth plane as karma, which carries us forward, bringing us ever closer to that essence of who we are as Divine Beings.

We can look back over the history of spirituality and find many master teachers who inform us of who we are. How did they know this, so long ago? Perhaps it was because karma had carried them through many lifetimes and experiences to a place of final knowing. They walked through the furnace of duality and came out of the other side much more aware of themselves as Divine Beings. Perhaps through the choice to engage in prayer and meditation in one life, they came into the next life full of the wisdom that they gained in the last. And they moved on from there to even greater awareness.

Of course, we can also look back through history and see many examples of despotism, genocide and horrific crimes. In our current duality trance state we look at the distinctions between the master teachers and the master criminals as evidence of "good" and "evil." But actually, they are all teachers. Through the law of projection, each of them both carried something and left something behind for us. Who knows what distorted energies these master criminals carried for the rest of us and because they carried it, protected us from having to, thus accelerating our evolution as One into Oneness? And who knows what wisdom, love and power those master teachers carried for the rest of us, what amazing Divine energy was hidden away from us as we projected it onto them? And because they carried it for us, they left behind a scent for us to follow, while giving us the fullness of time in which to experience duality. We *are* all One.

Ultimately karma will be the energy that will bring about the second coming. Now there's a sentence that declares the Oneness of East and West! Yes, karma. The second coming is not the return of one great master teacher. If it was, it would just mean more duality. More of our thinking that one man is separate from the others. One man is greater than others. One man can be Divine while the rest of us while away in our separateness, dying to get into heaven. Rather, the second coming is the ultimate fulfillment of the duality trance state.

Once duality has had its full run, once we have experienced all that duality can give us, we will find that there is more—much, much more—that cannot be explained by duality. We will, at that time, begin to understand, in a whole new light, our experiences with what has come to be called "altered states of consciousness." Many have experienced these "states" through meditation, Tai Chi, QiGong, yoga or other such means—some even imprudently seeking them through illegal drug use—in which they found themselves in some completely new kingdom of awareness, only to return momentarily to the ego-consciousness of duality. Some today even try to "bliss out" by staying in those altered states for longer and longer periods of time in order to escape the dull horror of the duality trance state. But when duality has finally done all that it can do, there will be no more "states"—just the ultimate truth of our Divine Beingness. At that point, we will not have to seek altered states of consciousness, nor will there be another reality waiting for us to return to it. We will have finally arrived at the only truth: Divine Oneness. We will have come, for the second time, to that awareness.

The first time was our original coming to planet earth as Divine Beings. It was because we so solidly knew who we were at that time that we could allow the "altered state" of duality consciousness. So, now, as the soul enters each life, solidly knowing itself as Divine, it can again agree to allow duality consciousness. But the ego, ego-state, body, mind, heart and life of each incarnation are the students of the soul, and because there is karma, the soul will ultimately give us the full lesson. And because karma works together with the law of attraction, we are attracted to and by the parents, the challenges and the potentialities that will fulfill the soul's intention for that lifetime. And the soul's intention is *always* fulfilled for each incarnation. Further, each individual consciousness that fully experiences itself as Divine Self, moves collective consciousness just that much closer to Self-realization, so that eventually all of us will awaken; we will come for a second time to know who we really are. Can you imagine an earth plane filled with egos that are One with the soul, of bodies that are one with the Divine? The intention that is karma is getting us there every single minute of time consciousness. And it is getting us there through the power of the next law.

The Law of Love

There is so much hate! So much violence! So much inequity! So much manipulation and power mongering! How can we possibly believe that there is a law of love? Well, whether we believe it or not is the choice we make. But the law is operative regardless.

The law of love says this: Every single thing that we do, say, feel and think ultimately shakes down to love. This means that even the most angry moment shakes down to love—indeed, even the most heinous crime ultimately shakes down to love. The law of love is the ability for one energy to convert to another. Here's an example from my own life about how that works.

My mother was a very frightened woman. She feared most people, didn't trust anyone and lived a life of silent aloneness. The result of this is that she raised me and my siblings with a kind of distant distrust and even distain. She flipped between periods of deep brooding rage and distant cold indifference. But she came across to many others as a warm and caring person—simply because she felt that she had to in order to get where she wanted to go in life. She was a very hard worker, and she was promoted rapidly and rose to the top levels of her field of nursing. She was highly respected and esteemed on the job.

Once, my siblings and I decided to throw our mother a surprise birthday party, with the help of one of her friends and coworkers. Many of her coworkers and employees came to that party and they all lined up to tell us that our mother was an "angel." Years later, my siblings and I talked about that day and how shocked we were to hear that our mother presented to the outside world such a very different picture of herself than the one we all saw. We were all thinking, "Who are you talking about? That's not my Mom!" All of that angelic love was given to others, not to her children who were waiting like hungry baby birds for her to come home and love us. So, how can I look at this and say that her actions toward us ultimately fall down to unconditional love?

Here's how that might work. Suppose that my mother and I chose this life with each other to mutually help each other to the next level of awareness. I don't know how I might have helped her to her next level, so let's keep it simple by making suppositions only about my end of that dynamic. Suppose as I grow up,

I repeatedly get attracted to and pick as partners cold indifferent people, some of whom also carry a secret brooding rage. After a while I might begin to "get it" that I've got some unfinished business with my mother. I might go to a therapist and begin to connect the dots between my mother, whom I loved desperately—though I'd told myself that I didn't care about her, because she didn't care about me—and the people with whom I'd fallen desperately in love.

First, what I begin to see is that I loved my mother, regardless of what she did. And then I begin to see that I loved these other people regardless of what they did. Then I begin to see that I loved myself enough to leave these uncaring and toxic people. Finally, I begin to see that my love for my mother, those old loves and myself is unconditional. And I learned all of that because I had been presented so many conditions to love.

Now, suppose that it is my karma—my soul's intention—to learn that I have the capacity for unconditional love. Would that mean that my mother and those old loves were all assisting me in getting to my ultimate goal? If that were true, wouldn't that mean that, in spite of how it appeared to me on the duality plane, on the plane of ultimate truth, they were actually giving me a loving gift? I say, yes.

So, what this means is that when we put the law of attraction together with the law of love what we can conclude is that everything, every circumstance, every encounter and every person is providing us with the energy and love to accomplish this life's goal. And this means that there is no utterly unloving act—regardless of how it looks from the duality trance state. But we might ask: Couldn't I have learned the same thing from people who also loved me unconditionally and taught me how to love unconditionally? Well, of course, I'll never know, because that is not what happened. But let's say, maybe. Maybe I would have learned the same thing if they had all loved me unconditionally and shown me the various ways in which I also loved unconditionally. But what *that* ultimately means is that regardless of what happens, I'm going to learn that I love unconditionally. Doesn't that still mean that everything ultimately is offering me the same tender lesson?

Well, it's true that I got it this time. I got the lesson. I get it. I have a capacity for unconditional love. Further, I now know that this capacity is in no wise special, for we all have the same capacity. It's just that this time, I know it. So, we might ask, what is going on when we don't seem to get the lesson? Can we then say that everything still comes down to love?

The law of karma, because it defines Divine intention, means that each lifetime has something specific to offer and we *will* get that specific thing. Because we've been taught the dualistic definition of karma, we believe that we can fail in one life and will need to fix that failure in another. But just because karma didn't give me what I got in *this* life, doesn't mean that it failed to give me what karma intended for *that* life. Rather, each life prior to this one gave me something specific *in preparation for* the gift I received in this life. And this life will in turn prepare me for something I'll get in another. But ultimately it is my soul's intention—my karma—to attain to full awareness of Divine Self. And the enormous and potent law of love is the power behind that karma. In fact, there is no greater gift than to assist each other toward full consciousness, and we are each giving that gift all day every day. This is what Jesus meant by the statement, found in John 15:13: "Greater love has no one than this, that one lay down his life for his friends." We have each one come here to lay down our lives for each other, as we live out incarnations that facilitate each other's Ultimate Consciousness.

And when the ultimate karma arrives for all of us in the form of the second coming to awareness of Divine Self, what will happen is that we will all be consumed in this amazing love. We will all look at the nowness of our previous attainment of wisdom through the duality trance state and we will laugh in utter joy at the power of transformative energies that were always being activated in our dualistic lives. What we thought was pain was just love. What we thought was heartbreak, was only love. And if we could activate that awareness in the now, we could begin to see our suffering today, as merely an altered state of awareness in which we see suffering, when actually it is always only love—for love is the very nature of Life.

The Law of Life

Coursing through the veins of our essence is a Life force that is more powerful, potent, passionate, joyous and peaceful than we can even imagine in our current duality trance state. It runs through everything as steady as a heartbeat. Have you ever wondered how it is that your heart keeps beating? Does it have a certain number of beats before it just quits? What energy pushes whatever other mechanisms in the body or brain that push the heart's rhythm? It is Life.

The tree of Life, the river of Life, these are the symbols we have used to understand this Life force. The Life force of a tree is in its roots, and the Life force of the roots is the nutrients it obtains from the earth. And the Life force of the earth is…? The Life force of the river is its source deep in the caverns of the earth. And the Life force of the earth is…? Isn't it true that we always come down to that question mark? Even when we go all the way down to the big bang theory, we still have to ask what caused the big bang.

In our currently dualistic trance state, we stop short of the ultimate questions, because some of our religions remind us that ultimacy means some kind of ultimate divide between heaven and hell, between earth and something else beyond it, between "good" and "evil." So, we just don't go there. Even those of us who are atheists very often stop short of these ultimate questions, because they lead to mysteries we cannot explain.

But when we get to the end of all of those questions what we find is Life. Life that presses upward toward hope like a tree toward the sun. Life that urges Life at all costs. Life that flows to the sea of Life. Life that continues even after we die. Life that gives Life, that moves Life, that carries Life: Life that is bigger than life—the dualistic view of Life—Life that is the power and thrust of all things. Life. This Life force is passionate, urgent, even pleading; it is the power of the ocean, the hurricane, the earthquake and the mountain, driving through us creating the power behind all of the other Universal laws. It is our deepest and truest origin.

But, duality has us thinking that we originate in sin. That we come from our genes, that we come only from a seed planted in our mothers. Duality makes us think that we keep ourselves alive because we strive after survival. But we don't survive because we are striving after survival. We survive because of this Life energy coursing through our veins. And we don't die.

We don't die. We go on to come back to follow the line of the soul's intention in the sand yet again. And we will continue to do so until all of us get it. We will live until we Live. And so as we wander though our lives looking for what it is that we'd like to attract, the Life force within us attracts Life. We are attracted to and attracted by all those things that bring us to awareness of this Life force that moves within and around us, certain of its power to carry us through life to Life.

What we can conclude then, is that every one of the other Universal laws interacts with the law of attraction. But our current understanding of the law of attraction comes from the perspective of the duality trance state in which we all live. And so we have reduced the law of attraction to that dualistic framework. We have reduced it to our power to change our thoughts, and thereby change our circumstances.

What this reduction implies is that we are supposed to have it differently. This thinking keeps us attached to outcomes, even as we are saying that we want to detach from outcomes. It has us coming at our life circumstances from the perspective of blame: Why can't I make this happen? It has us holding our egos accountable for matters of the soul.

When we realize that the soul is always in charge, we come at the law of attraction from an entirely different perspective. One in which every single circumstance, relationship, encounter, and inner conflict is giving us the gift of Life through an harmonious interaction between the law of attraction, and all of the other Universal laws, the laws of love, karma, now, choice, visibility and invisibility, duality, One, and even projection. We are all in a collective and individual process in which we are discovering again, actually remembering, who we are. These laws are all working together to get us there. So, rather than looking at our life's circumstances as not good enough, we can now genuinely say, "My life circumstances have been absolutely essential to get me to where I am today in my consciousness evolution and now, let me go yet deeper." And as we look at all of the orchestral movement of these laws in concert, we come to understand that it is not our thoughts that must change, but rather the depths to which we are willing to take our consciousness; for it is that willingness that will get us into the flow.

9

Getting in the Flow

Okay, so now we understand that the true law of attraction is the draw to and from those situations, persons, places, things, etc. which will bring us clearly and essentially to the power of Ultimate Consciousness of Divine Self. And we now also know that every other Universal law is working to bring about that same reality. But how do we get into that flow?

The most basic part of the process of getting into the flow is coming to understand that we are already in that flow. There is no way to dispute Universal law. We may be able to find a place of denial in our psyches, so that we don't allow ourselves to know that we are all on the same journey, but we *are* all on the same journey. Just as gravity works all around our little anti-gravity chambers—even holding down the chamber itself, so the true law of attraction works all around our little spaces of denial. We cannot disobey these laws.

We are always attracted to and being attracted by the Divine Self, in all things, situations, circumstances, bodies and lives, toward that Ultimate Consciousness. No matter what we do or don't do, no matter how many so-called "mistakes" we make, no matter how "bad" we've been, no matter what role we've lived, no matter what—we are always moving steadily toward the Ultimate Consciousness of Divine Self. This is what is meant by the statement—found in the New Testament letters from Paul—that all things work for good (Romans 8:28), a truth found in some other ancient sacred texts as well.

Because we still live in the duality trance state most of us believe that the "bad" things and the "mistakes" that we make will always land us in misery. But if we look at ours and the lives of others around us we know that this is not true. Just as we've had many worrisome, frightening and even so-called "negative" thoughts that amounted to nothing, we've made many mistakes and have done many things we later regret that held no other consequence, for ourselves or others, beyond our regret. There is no cause and effect relative to the "goodness" or "badness" the "rightness" or "wrongness" of our choices. Sometimes there are consequences for our choices, but this doesn't mean that the choices were "wrong." And though there may be rewards for some choices, that doesn't make them "right." Jesus said this best in Matthew 5:44-45:

> But I say to you, love your enemies, and pray for those who persecute you in order that you may be sons of your Father who is in heaven; for He causes His sun to rise on the evil and the good and sends rain on the righteous and the unrighteous.

Traditional interpretations look only at the advice to pray for our enemies. But there is much more to this statement, for he is clearly saying that the reason we should pray for our enemies is that there is no direct consequence to being bad or good. This insight renders irrelevant our original intention for inventing the good/bad dichotomy—which was to draw down the "good" rewards and forestall the "bad" (including the enemies) as a way of dealing with the prospect of suffering. Beyond that, the statement also clearly informs us that we are all in the same boat together.

Many who espouse the current understanding of the law of attraction swear by another statement supposedly made by Jesus:

> Do not be deceived, God is not mocked; for whatever a man sows, this he will also reap.

But this statement was never made by Jesus. It was made by the writer of Galatians (6:7), who is thought by most to be Paul. Jesus, unlike Paul, seems to have understood that we do not always reap what we sow, nor do we always sow what is reaped. He even alludes to this same theme, albeit on a different topic, when he says in John 4: 37-38:

> For in this case the saying is true, "One sows, and another reaps." I sent you to reap that for which you have not labored....

The philosophy that we deserve for "bad" things to happen to us when we've made "mistakes" or done "bad" things prevents us from seeing that even these things can work together to bring us into full awareness of the Divine Self. It prevents us from asking, "What is the gift under my regretful action?" Or, "How is 'goodness' keeping me from living the truth?" It prevents us from being able to see how it is that even a lifetime filled with what we would normally call "evil" can bring us to full understanding of what it is like to live so very far away from our own authenticity—an understanding we can carry with us into the next incarnation. It prevents us from noticing that even a lifetime filled with so-called "good deeds" can actually be a life of show-and-tell, that has nothing whatsoever to do with authentic kindness or compassion. It prevents us from understanding that Life is not something that must be deserved, or earned. Rather, Life chose this life for us, just as we chose this life for Life. It prevents us from seeing karma for what it is—the soul's intention that we continue to evolve toward that final destination of Ultimate Consciousness.

Let's consider this issue from its worst possible angle. Let's say that Dean is a sociopathic murderer. Most of us would simply write Dean off as "evil" and in need of either the death penalty or life in prison. First, yes, Dean does need to be kept far away from society, so that he will not harm others. While prison and the death penalty are not the best of all possible options, they do seem to be a part of how we are responding to the dilemma of the Deans in this world, and we can agree that if he gets caught, one of these two options is likely and preferable to just allowing him to continue his killing spree. So, our discussion of what is going on with Dean does not imply that he should just be allowed to "get away with it." But does that mean that we should categorize him as "evil" and be done with any further thought about it? I do often find that such categorization is a method we use to avoid having to deal with the much more difficult but enlightening possibilities inherent in the problem of "evil." Such avoidance is meant to create great psychic distance between Dean and the rest of us, because we fear that seriously contemplating him will somehow magically give him more power or even make us somehow like him.

The truth is that there are probably three operative elements in Dean's case. The first is that he probably pre-verbally identified as an "evil" person, based on dilemmas presented by his biological parents or primary caregivers. My theory is that such preverbal identifications create what we call sociopathy. Second, he probably has *alexithymia*—a deep and firm compartmentalization of his emotions, which makes it impossible to be aware of, process or verbalize such normal responses as affection, empathy and remorse. And third, he is carrying the projection of "evil" first for his family-of-origin and then for all of us. He might, in fact, be carrying a projection of "badness" for the entire world, while simultaneously learning what it is like to live so alienated from a sense of connection to his own nature. It's not terribly hard for us to accept the first two of these operative elements, but this idea of projection is much more difficult for us to swallow. Yet all one has to do to look for evidence of the power of this particular projection is to acknowledge the enormous popularity of the HBO series *The Sopranos* and the Showtime series, *Dexter*. We are actually rooting for the serial killers and mafia men in these shows, for not only do we find some redeeming characteristics in them, but they are able to express without remorse all those things we'd secretly like to express. They carry our projections well, do they not?

But it is extremely difficult for us to wrap our minds around this notion that Dean is not "evil." We will resist this idea with tooth and nail. So, in order to facilitate further understanding of this concept we need to look at it similarly to the way we watch *The Sopranos* and *Dexter*. We need to see it for the drama it is. If it is really true that no one dies and that all of our suffering is useful to move us ever closer to the Divine nature, then Dean's life and the lives and families of those he wounds or kills are all part of the drama of the duality trance state through which we are all working toward the unification of Ultimate Consciousness. On the duality plane—the origin of our suffering—this drama causes a great deal of pain, anger, grief and other forms of torment. But on the soul plane, we are getting to know who we are at ever deeper levels. In other words, on the soul plane all forms of suffering are but lights along the pathway. Regardless of the intensity of the crisis—each crisis is meant, by both the psyche and the soul, to bring consciousness further down the pathway toward Divine Self awareness. And regardless of which identity we choose, be it Pollyanna or Serial Killer, it is meant to help us to move ultimately, lifetime after lifetime, down the pathway to authenticity. *We are only in this play because we are trying to be real.* And once we become real, the entire Universe becomes just that much more real as well.

Does this notion mock our suffering? No, in fact it is the very basis of our suffering, for we suffer to the exact degree to which we are attached to the drama, instead of to the Ultimate Consciousness behind all drama, the Divine Self. If I am the family member of one of the sociopath's victims, my suffering will not conclude until I make some kind of peace with it. It will not stop when the sociopath is executed. It will not stop when "justice" is done. It only stops when I make peace with it. We don't do the inner work of making such peace without at least touching the hem of the garment of the soul. And so we see the drama of duality played out on a stage that enables those on that stage to have an experience that alchemically changes them. These experiences work to ignite the fires of realization and remembrance of who we are, in the same way that rubbing two sticks together will start a literal fire. Only experience has this power. And we are going to need all kinds of experiences in order to fully encounter all of the possibilities of duality.

When we bring this up out of the realms of the most horrific, to the more ordinary kinds of suffering, what we see is that if I choose a life, for example, in which I seem hopelessly compelled to repeat the same mistakes again and again, frustrating everyone who loves me and wishes for me a better life, it might be in order to fully experience in this lifetime, such compulsion and blindness. And I have this experience, not only for myself, but also for all of those in the world who need my experience to impact their own, for all of those people who are projecting their powerless compulsions onto me and for all of the rest of creation. To earth consciousness, my life might look like a terrible waste of flesh and bone, and then I die. But to my soul, my life accomplished exactly what it was supposed to accomplish.

What would it be like to try to find my soul in the bottom of a bottle of Vodka? What would it be like to feel so alienated from my own soul that I spend a lifetime enraged at the world? What would it be like to live in a perpetual dark night of the soul, through a devastating mental illness? What would it be like to be hit with several crises in my life that offer me the opportunity to wake up slowly to who I really am as a Divine Self? What would it be like to live a life filled with wealth and ease? There is no answer to these questions except to "be like" that alienation, that desperate search for soul in alcohol, that perpetual dark night, the effect of those crises on me and that wealth and ease. We simply must have all of these experiences and more in order to co-create a Universe in which these experiences are no longer necessary—a Universe in which the question of duality has finally been answered.

There is a passage in the "Revelation to John" that gives us a perfect analogy to these experiences:

> Behold, I stand at the door and knock; if anyone hears My voice and opens the door, I will come in to him, and will dine with him, and he with Me (3:20).

These experiences assist the Divine Self in attracting our full attention. Every single experience of our lives is a knock at the door of our psyches to open up to full awareness of who we really are. Once we open the door the Divine Self enters our consciousness and earth consciousness is then merged with Divine Self, earth body is then ensouled with its full empowerment, and earth objects are seen for their truest nature. Each person who opens that door, who becomes fully aware of Divine Self within, brings the entirety of collective earth consciousness that much closer to Ultimate Consciousness. Because we are all One, such an energetic shift in the consciousness of even one person, sends a small but impactful vibration all around the world so that everyone else's consciousness shifts to some degree. This is the true law of attraction in action.

In the prophet Isaiah's book (55:11), we read this:

> So shall My word be which goes forth from My mouth; it shall not return to Me empty, without accomplishing what I desire, and without succeeding in the matter for which I sent it.

If we think of "My word" as it is described in the introduction to the Gospel of John, it removes the religious dogma from this statement. John's words in the first few verses of his book are very similar to the words found in the Bhagavad Gita. John says (1-5):

> In the beginning was the Word and the Word was with God, and the Word was God. He was in the beginning with God. All things came into being by Him, and apart from Him nothing came into being that has come into being. In Him was life, and the life was the light of men. And the light shines in the darkness, and the darkness did not comprehend it.

The Bhagavad Gita says this:

> 10: 20: I am the true Self in the heart of every creature, Arjuna, and the beginning, middle, and end of their existence (Easwaran 1985, 2007, 185).*

> 9: 10-11: Under my watchful eye the laws of nature take their course. Thus is the world set in motion; thus the animate and the inanimate are created. The immature do not look beyond the physical appearances to see my true nature as the Lord of all creation (174).*

> 10:39: I am the seed that can be found in every creature, Arjuna; for without me nothing can exist, neither animate nor inanimate (189).*

The Word then can be seen as the soul, the Divine Self, Ultimate Consciousness. And it will not return to its origin, at the end of any single lifetime, empty. This means that regardless of what we are thinking in our dualistic mindset of earth consciousness, there is not one single failed life. Not one. The soul within us is always attracting us to itself—and it cannot fail.

The dualistic mindset wants us to believe that we can not only be separate from our own Divine nature, but that because this is so, we can fail to live up to that nature's standards. And in Christian thought, not only can we fail, but we can displease the soul so mightily that we send ourselves to eternal alienation from it. The soul, in this case, is projected out of the body/mind of humanity and onto a Superpower, with strangely human characteristics, and who, because we have so failed "him," would send us to this eternal alienation.

But if the law of One is real, then there is not now, nor has there ever been such a separation. We cannot be separated from our own essential nature! That essential nature is constantly active in our lives, rubbing the two sticks of individual consciousness and Ultimate Consciousness together, so that in some incarnation down the way, the flame will ignite until all is consumed in the ultimate love and grace of Divine Self. And each experience we have in any single incarnation moves us closer to ignition time.

Do we really believe that something as puny and insignificant as an ego-state—a mask and a costume—could be more powerful than the Divine Self? Do we really believe that the power of earth consciousness—which is blind, deaf, and dumb to the reality of Life—could be more powerful than the soul who is "the beginning, middle, and end of creation" and who is "life and the life was the light of men?"

While it is true that we live here on this earth blinded by earth consciousness, we have not been left here alone. The soul, the Divine Self has not left us to our own devices, but is in fact, always in charge. It uses all the laws discussed in the previous chapter to accomplish its ends, utilizing our experiences, whether "positive" or "negative" to bring us to Ultimate Consciousness. We will not, cannot fail to finally arrive.

When we surrender to that fact, it is a bit like surrendering to the beating of our own hearts. On some level we are always so surrendered, but on another, waking up to such surrender is a conscious act. And that act is accomplished through the power of realization. We simply begin to let the idea of the Divine Self gestate into realization. While it is true that we cannot push such an awakening, any more than we can push a river, it is also true that there are some ways that we can nudge the earth just a little to crack open and let the river of Life spring forth. Meditation is one of those ways. But we are not talking about structuring meditation along the lines of a more or less rigid framework in which we don't move or think, or we deliberately visualize something.

The thing I personally love about meditation is that it is not structured at all. That, in my view, is why it gets us so clearly into the flow. Meditation is a gentle inward look, that falls down under the shadows of thought, past the regions of emotions, while noticing and attending to each, and down into the deep inner regions of Self. As we just quietly notice, without judgment, our thoughts and emotions, we begin to feel the presence of the Self. This doesn't mean that we will not dally with a given thought or emotion. In fact, it may be that an intense emotion must come forth and call for expression. But what it does mean is that we are more or less in the observer mode. We are mindful of the thought and the emotion, even experiencing both, but still holding to the position of the audience, the observer.

Practicing such meditation on a daily basis gets us more and more familiar with the inner terrain. The more familiar we become with that inner terrain, the more comfortable we are in walking it. The more comfortable we are in walking it, the more friendly we are with how certain things feel. For example, what does intuition feel like, as opposed to fear? What does this thought feel like, or that belief? What happens in my body when I feel afraid? What happens in my body when I feel bliss? These and more are questions asked and answered through the practice of meditation.

But surrender is the primary essence of the flow. The word "surrender" carries with it a load of fundamentalist connotation, so let's clarify what this word means for the purposes of this book. Surrender is not a state of defeat. Nor does it imply that we are going to become enraptured in some ethereal state of bliss. Nor does it mean that we are saved and going to heaven. Surrender means that we realize that even the greatest strength, wisdom, intelligence and bravery of the ego or ego-state, is not enough, *by itself,* to bring us to the Divine Self. In fact, it is the Divine Self that brings us to full awareness of the Divine Self. So, what do we do when we come to this profound realization? We land full-weight on the Divine Self to carry us.

Surrender is also a form of acceptance. All those bargains of which we spoke in Chapter 4 come to a screeching halt in the face of surrender. Acceptance is a new perception of reality in which we realize that our circumstances and our lives are valuable just as they are—they are "good enough." That doesn't mean that we won't change things as we choose, but that we do not dismiss a certain reality simply because it doesn't fit the schema with which we've identified. In fact, such acceptance allows room for realization of the flow that is the masterful blending of ego and Divine Self in Life. Bargaining denies us that beautiful realization.

Such acceptance is surrender because it surrenders us to now. Now, here, where we are, what we are doing, who we are looking at in the mirror. Now in this moment, in which both suffering and glory are occurring simultaneously. Now in this challenge to go deeper, look higher, see more. Now. Such acceptance sees thoughts and feelings—whether "negative" or "positive"—as part of the experience that is our grand teacher, the soul's grand plan for this life even as it exists in the duality trance state. It sees that even in the duality trance state, in which we mostly live, we are having this amazing experience with life in which we can feel the depths of sorrow and the heights of joy. This awareness is a kind of allowance. It is the ego giving permission for Life to carry us where it carries us. This doesn't mean that all struggle will immediately cease. It only means that we begin by seeing the struggle as part of the experience that will bring us, through the true law of attraction, to the Divine Self. But paradoxically, such vision means that the need to struggle is greatly reduced and ultimately consumed in Divine Self.

Surrender fully recognizes the force behind all things. Surrender recognizes that, as Jesus put it, "I can do nothing on my own initiative." This means that we can do and do and do; we can strive to change our thoughts and our feelings and even our behavior, but it amounts to nothing if it is not also done by Divine Self. Striving is a bargain that says IF I can get myself to change, THEN I'll be a "good" person and will get those rewards, or THEN my life will be better or easier, etc. Surrender, on the other hand, fully understands that all of our striving is going to amount to more nothing—for that is all that we can do of our own initiative. But the "Father," as Jesus called this river of Life flowing through us, is the initiator and the doer. Surrender to that force is a clear realization that we are not, even with the mightiest of our ego/personality power, going to make something happen that the force of Life within does not want to happen. The passage in the prophet Zechariah's book says it best (4:6):

> Not by might, not by power, but by my Spirit, says the Lord.

The current understanding of the law of attraction tells us that IF we just work hard enough on "positive" thinking and vision boards, THEN we will make our dreams come true, eliminating "negative" circumstances from our lives. But surrender acknowledges that even the difficult circumstances in which we often find ourselves are not separate from the Life force within, which will ultimately bring us home to Divine Self. That does not mean that we just curl up into a fetal position and suck our thumbs. It means that we realize that whatever true changes occur, they will be the result of the power of that Life force, the Divine Self. We can join forces with that Divine Self by surrendering to it. Such surrender is definitely recognized by the Divine Self. Self knows when the door has been opened, and will definitely walk on through to "dine with us."

We deny the power of this absolute force when we say that we are the ones who have to make it happen, in and of the power of earth consciousness—even as we are renunciating ego. In order to attain what is of real Life we must be aligned with the real Life force within us. But this does not deny the power of that Life force that continues to operate in our lives *whether or not* we are consciously aligned with it.

Personally, one of the most important periods of enlightenment in my life came on the heels of a deep depression. I began to realize that the power of the river of Life was not stopped up—depriving me of its abundant flow. Rather it was an amazing force, and had in fact kept me alive through some deadly times. But I'd been projecting my own feeling of helplessness onto the flow of Life, by assuming that if I didn't make it happen, it simply was not going to happen. And I felt powerless to make it happen. That whole belief system for me was based on the idea, internalized from my dysfunctional family-of-origin, that no one cared about me. Not only did they not care, but they would do whatever they could to stand in the way of my happiness. So devoured was I in that belief that even my image of the Divine was swallowed whole by it.

But I came to understand, through my own suffering, that the Divine Self within me was not only completely active at all times, even when I didn't know it, but was also gently guiding me over the years to join it in a Holy Marriage of body, mind, soul, consciousness and unconsciousness, left with right, up with down and all around. The only thing standing in the way of my happiness was my perception about life. Surrender realizes this fact and yields to wholeness.

But it must be said that this surrender is not the same as the traditional concept of "God's will." This theory is that God—

defined, again, as an external superhuman entity with not so superhuman character traits—has a certain plan for our lives. According to this paradigm, we are meant to surrender to God's will *instead of* our own, because our will is "bad" and God's will is "good," even when it doesn't feel good. Based on this theory, many well-intended comforters offer, as their chief comfort, the platitude "It was God's will," in the face of horrific tragedy. And I have yet to meet a single individual who has been truly comforted by these words, for they lack empathy and are actually quite dismissive. And based on that same theory, we have young people finding a "calling to do God's will" in feelings of intense and miserable guilt, which actually stem from a false identity, but are defined by misguided spiritual leaders as saintly "conviction."

Divine Self is internal. It is the truest essence of who we are. So, surrendering is surrendering to our own truest intentions—for in fact, there is no way to truly surrender to anything else. How could we, in truth, surrender to something or someone alien or unknown to ourselves? No. Surrendering to something other than our own truest essence is an intellectual endeavor filled with all manner of repression and denial. And we need not fear surrender to our truest essence, for *Divine Self does not want anything for us that we, at our deepest essence, do not want for ourselves.*

So, both meditation, which explores the inner terrain from the perspective of the observer, and surrender, which accepts our reality without bargaining by realizing the Divine Self in it, are two of the chief processes Divine Self uses to get us into the flow. And both work together quite harmoniously. They move us to a place in which, as we walk through our lives, we are in a perpetual state of realization, and a perpetual communion with the deeper aspects of ourselves. They put us into the walk in which we are not the initiators of our lives, even as we are constantly initiating our lives. They put us into the effortless effort of the flow. They bring us to that essential Divine Self, the soul, the unwounded, unbound, limitless, fearless, power of absolute love.

Just one more question. Why would we *not* surrender to that?

* From *The Bhagavad Gita,* translated by Eknath Easwaran, founder of the Blue Mountain Center of Meditation, copyright 1985, 2007; reprinted by permission of Nilgiri Press, P. O. Box 256, Tomales, CA 94971, www.easwaran.org.

10

I AM

In the Old Testament book of the Christian Bible or the Torah of the Tanakh, we read the story of the Jewish Exodus from Egypt, which began with Moses' calling, through a spirit in a burning bush, to lead the Israelites to the Promised Land. When Moses asked of this Spirit, "whom shall I say sent me," the answer he was given was this (Exodus 3:14):

> God said to Moses, "I AM WHO I AM"; and He said, "Thus you shall say to the sons of Israel, 'I AM has sent me to you.'"

Sounds a little funny, don't you think? Can you imagine what the people were thinking when he came back to them and said "I AM has sent me to you?" I'm thinking that if I were in that crowd I might assume that Moses was saying something like, "I have sent myself to you."

Turns out, as we study the original Hebrew language, that is exactly what he meant. This language tells us that I AM who I AM literally means *To BE is/was/will be To BE,* translated into Jehovah, which means *the existing one*. The phrase *the existing one* originates in the infinitive *to desire.* So, Moses was actually saying something like this: "My desire, that is my deepest existence, my very Beingness sent me to you."

Our deepest existence is the very essence of desire. It is the longing to BE. And that desire, that Being is Divine in nature. Such desire does not go unquenched. It is a fire that will not go out. It is constantly creating Being from its desire to Be. And this process cannot be stopped.

Our current understanding of the law of attraction is so puny in the face of such raw power. At its core, this power is love of Life, for there is no desire without love. In fact, in 1 John 4:16 we are told that the Divine essence *is* love. If the Divine essence is both love and desire, then we come to understand the two seemingly different terms as synonymous. And it is from this remarkable union of love and desire that we are made. In our most essential nature, then, we are the fire of love whose burning urgency will perpetually accomplish what it desires. No puny little "positive" or "negative" thought is even going to come close to measuring up to the amazing thrust of such awesome power.

But if we believe that at the core base of ourselves we are pure desire to Be, which is constantly creating more and more Being, then we know the *true* law of attraction. We know that this raw force within us cannot be stopped from attracting all that is necessary to bring us to full Beingness. Ultimate Consciousness is simply consciousness of Beingness, the Divine Self, the I AM. Our deepest desire, as individuals and as a collective, is to bring consciousness to bear on the essence of who we are. And, who we are is so much more than what we have.

That said, however, what we have—those things, people, places and situations that we say we own—are the desire to Be *in form*. Even if what we have is a "little ole piece of a car and a hunk of bread," as they say in the South, the desire to Be can be found there. This doesn't mean that we are to just accept that this is all that we can have, but it does mean that everything we have is part of the desire to Be.

From the Old Testament and the Ketuvim of the Tanakh in Psalms Twenty-Three, we read this beautiful affirmation of the above assertion:

> The Lord is my Shepherd, I shall not want.

If desire to Be is my shepherd, desire never goes wanting. We do not, cannot lack for anything, for the desire to be is constantly living out its desire through Being.

Wait just a minute now! Am I saying that all of the starvation in the world is a result of this desire to be? If the cattle on a thousand hills are mine, then how is it that we have starvation anywhere on planet earth? Remember that we said that in order to consciously attain what is of real Life we must be *consciously aligned* with the Life force within us? As long as we live in the duality trance state in which we fully believe in and identify with something other than that real Life force within us, we are going to live that out. When, however, we begin to surrender to the flow of Life energy within us, to consciously be shepherded by this deep desire to Be, we will no longer believe that we can be split-off from our deepest Selves, and we will live in full view of what belongs to us.

The process that started with the onset of our journey here on planet earth is one in which we, as a collective, absolutely must encounter and experience every single shred of duality and come to conclude that duality is not, nor has it ever been true. Currently, we are still at a place in that historical journey, in which many of us yet believe that to acknowledge ourselves to be One with the Divine is to blaspheme or to be insane. We still live in a world in which we are largely superstitious about living and spend whole lifetimes bargaining with realities we just don't want to consider. We still live in a world in which the fundamentalism of several different religions keeps us stuck hiding behind our fears and holding on to all manner of irrational, doubly-binding and even suffocating beliefs.

And yet, as we've already seen, at the base of our fundamentals, in the mysterious mystical elements of most religions, we find this one central theme: At our deepest essence, we are all Divine Beings. Yet many do not study these religions at their deep mystical levels. Many of us, because we are still living in the duality trance state, stay on the surface of spirituality, while barely attending to any religion. This surface relationship gives us not much more than a rabbit's foot to hold to when we are scared. Beyond that we live only in duality.

Further, as long as we live in a world in which money is the bargaining tool we use to keep safe from the wolves at the door, because of the law of projection, we will have poverty and starvation. As long as we live in a dualistic world in which people can identify as "evil," we will have serial killing and genocide. As long as we live in a world that is shepherded by duality, we will have what duality offers.

But when we awaken to the truth of who we are, then we no longer want. The cattle on a thousand hills *are* ours. We have clothing finer than any Solomon ever wore. We have put first the kingdom of heaven and all of these things have been added unto us. In other words, our Being has increased to contain them. The seeker has been sought and found.

Think of it. The essence of who we are is desire to Be. Powerful desire that will not be stopped until it has what it desires. Is there any greater law of attraction than this? We can absolutely get in alignment with this awesome power. But we might need to re-think the law of attraction as we currently understand it, in order to do so.

The current understanding of the law of attraction has many of us thinking that we are meant to "improve" ourselves by, as we've said, getting rid of ego or eliminating the garbage from the shadow or thinking "positive" and vision boarding. But as we've now seen the *real* law of attraction has to do with surrender, rather than self-improvement. It has to do with merging into Oneness all aspects of the Self, rather than "getting rid of" or "eliminating" anything. It has to do with acceptance of and surrender to who we *really* are. It has to do with Ultimate Consciousness, Divine Self, the river of Life, the desire to Be.

The process of Divine Self is one in which we may begin to accept ourselves as One with the Divine. This may take some time since we have been so inculcated with the duality trance state. But we can begin, as we said in the previous chapter, to meditate and listen to that deep desire to Be. This can become a daily practice, just simply sitting with our own deep inner essence. In fact, it can become such a powerful part of our daily practice that we begin not only to sit with it, but to walk with it, so that even as we are busy with our days, we are still present with our deepest essence.

As we are spending time within, we can learn to discern the fine lines of distinction between the desire that is the Divine Self and the desire that is compulsion. Compulsion is fear-based and is often a bargain, such as, IF I have that, THEN I can be that. Desire is pure joy. It is the deepest wish we have to unite every aspect of ourselves into One Being. Desire does not reach outside of the Self to attain or have, but finds all of its needs and wants met within an ever-expanding Self that is always creating more Being.

Finally, we may begin to live fully surrendered to alignment with the Divine Self. Again this doesn't mean that there was ever a time when we were literally out of alignment, but that we now know and receive our truest Self as the initiator of our lives. This means that we will not be seeking from the outside world, but we will go within and receive the gifts of Divine Self from within and give them to our worlds, as opposed to trying to drag the externals home for dinner.

This is all about vision. We will begin to see ourselves in the flow we are already in, and in so doing we become congruent with the Self. But we don't see the Divine Self while we are waiting for the world to give us what we think we want. Instead, we see it by tuning in and listening to the silent roar of the river of Life within. We see it by looking beneath the surface reality to the greater reality taking place even as we are looking. We see it when we look under every event, circumstance, health issue, every thought and feeling, for the essence, the energy of Divine Self. No experience is complete until we've experienced all of its dimensions. When we only allow ourselves to experience the duality dimension, we simply do not know the whole experience.

But wholeness is not something we can strive to attain. Rather we may choose to enter these energies of the Divine Self through the door of surrender. We may choose to trust the paradox that one can only experience Divine Self by experiencing Divine Self. We may choose to trust the process of unfolding awareness that allows us that experience. Rather than straining at the gnat of experience, we may choose to cease striving and sit with the reality that the Divine Self *is* actually within us, in fact it is the truest essence of us. And as we do, we are opening the door to the knock, and the Divine Self will come through, making itself apparent to us, for:

> Those who wait for the Lord will gain new strength; they will mount up with wings like eagles, they will run and not get tired, they will walk and not become weary (Isaiah 40:31).

Our current understanding of the law of attraction, based on the duality trance state, has us attempting to bridge the seeming gap between ourselves and the Divine by our own efforts. The method of rejoining our awareness with the Divine described in Isaiah above is one in which the Divine bridges the gap because we are waiting. We sit with the fact that we are Divine at our truest essence and the Divine comes to inform us that yes, indeed, this is so. And then we rise up, we transcend the duality trance state so that we no longer see it as our source, but rather are enlivened by the Divine within us. From here, we begin to operate from effortless effort, in which we are carried through our daily lives by the power and grace of the Divine Self. And from there, that same power and grace gives to our external lives the creations made within.

We cannot come to a clear definition of the Divine, without an individual and profound journey into union with the Divine. In spite of that fact, much of traditional thought would lead us to believe that, though we are separate from the Divine, we can define "Him" in very specific terms. But how can we possibly define an energy from which we believe we have been completely separate from the beginning of time? Yet our traditions have held onto those definitions with rabid attachment—even to the point of killing millions of innocents because they didn't agree.

This is spiritual double-speak at its worst. How can we define something we cannot experience because it lives on the other side of some invisible chasm? No, if we are going to understand the Divine, we must have a depth experience with the Divine. Many mystics have done just that—and, regardless of their religious persuasion, they have all come away from those experiences both transformed and informed. And while none of them have given us a literal definition of the mystery, they have told us that we are One with the Divine. We cannot find such depth experiences through the reading of a book—even this one—or by listening to a sermon, or a wise guru. Though external experiences do impact us, it is only when the inner Self meets the essence of that experience that we are truly influenced.

We have many external voices now telling us how we should go about establishing "a connection" with the Divine. And so this book does not intend to be yet another one of those external voices that says if you follow steps one, two and three, you will have arrived. This book is meant to offer some information that might help to further our collective and individual sacred journeys into the Divine Self. But the journey must belong to each individual. Each one of us has his or her own unique path to take and part of the amazing mystery of living is that I cannot know yours.

Meanwhile, because of our current connections to each other through the internet, TV, radio and cell phones, we are catching up with our own history. We are beginning to hear the voices of those who have delved into the mystery of their own Divine nature, voices which were previously only heard by their students, or by their cloistered readers. East and West have begun to link theories about religion and the Divine. The Bhagavad Gita, the Qu'ran, the forbidden and then lost books of the Nag Hammadi Library and other sacred texts have now been read and digested by many who hail from much more traditional Western religions. Many are meeting in interfaith efforts to resolve the conflicts between the various religions. Things are changing. And even as they are, there are many holding on even tighter to the old paradigms in fear of the oncoming change.

But the desire that *is* the Divine nature within us, *will* accomplish what it came to accomplish. It will continue to attract to us and be attracted to all things, people, circumstances, events, etc., which will bring us ever closer, through the process of experience, to our truest nature. And as we evolve ever closer, we will expand to include more and more of the Life energy that is desire in form.

It is time now for us to revise our understanding of the law of attraction to a much less dualistic format than the one to which we've previously been educated. We no longer have to walk the straight and narrow path of "positive" thinking that excludes all "negative" thinking *so that* we can have what we want in life. We no longer need to struggle and strive to clear out the shadow *in order* to hurry up and make our dreams come true. Rather, we can surrender to the reality of ourselves as Divine Self. We can begin to receive the deeper essence of our Beingness as the truth of our nature. We can begin to trust Oneness as the truth of the entire universe. We can begin to watch as Divine Self attracts greater and greater awareness of Divine Self in our lives. We can explore deeper and deeper regions of Self, coming closer and closer to full awareness of the river of Life running through the awesome terrain of the inner Being. We can kneel to drink of that water, lapping it up without the use of cupped hands, to quench our lifelong thirst, finally diving right in, soaking it up, swimming and playing as we are carried by it to all of Life. In so doing we will expand the form of our bodies to include formlessness, allowing LIFE to course through our veins like new wine in new wine skins—for I AM makes all things new. And as we do that we will simultaneously expand formlessness to include form. In so doing, we will enlarge who we are to take in and contain all that already belongs to us as Divine Self. There in the flow of Life, all of "these things" are added to us through the expansion of awareness that is the receipt of Divine Self. At last, form will be united with formlessness in our individual lives, impacting the collective, the earth and the entire universe with the amazing energy of that shift.

And we are, each and all, the valiant co-creators of this astounding new universe.

Works Cited

Brown, James Robert, "Thought Experiments", *The Stanford Encyclopedia of Philosophy (Fall 2009 Edition)*, Edward N. Zalta (ed.) http://plato.stanford.edu/archives/fall2009/entries/thought-experiment/ (Accessed 4/6/10)

Carl Jung Resources. "The Concept of the Collective Unconscious." Carl Jung Resources, 2009.
http://www.carl-jung.net/collective_unconscious.html
(Accessed 04/24/10)

Chang, Larry, ed. *Wisdom for the Soul: Five Millennia of Prescriptions for Spiritual Healing,* Washington D.C.: Gnosophia Publishers, 2006.

Easwaran, Eknath, Translator, *The Bhagavad Gita.* Tomales, CA: *Nilgiri Press,* 1985, 2007

Erickson, Lisa. "Is the Law of Attraction Buddhist?" *BellaOnline.* Minerva WebWorks LLC, 2010.
http://www.bellaonline.com/articles/art34035.asp
(Accessed 4/23/ 10)

Merriam-Webster's Collegiate® Dictionary, 11th Edition. "Thought." Merriam-Webster Inc., 2010.
http://www.merriam-webster.com/dictionary/thought
(Accessed 3/6/10)

Merriam-Webster's Collegiate® Dictionary, 11th Edition. "Think." Merriam-Webster Inc., 2010.
http://www.merriam-webster.com/dictionary/think
(Accessed 3/6/10)

Schucman, Helen. *A Course in Miracles: Combined Volume.* Mill Valley, CA: The Foundation of Inner Peace, 2007.

Smith, Andrew Phillip. *The Gospel of Philip: Annotated and Explained.* Skylight Paths Publishing, 2005.

Zodhiates, Spiros, ed. *The Hebrew-Greek Key Study Bible: New American Standard.* Chattanooga, TN: AMG International, Inc.,1984 and 1990.